# Perfect
# Decisions

GW00705998

# Perfect
# Decisions

ALL YOU NEED
TO GET IT RIGHT
FIRST TIME

ANDREW LEIGH

ARROW
BUSINESS BOOKS

Published by Arrow Books in 1993

1 3 5 7 9 10 8 6 4 2

© Andrew Leigh

First published by
Arrow Books Limited
20 Vauxhall Bridge Road, London SW1V 2SA

Random House Australia (Pty) Limited
20 Alfred Street, Milsons Point, Sydney
New South Wales 2061, Australia

Random House New Zealand Limited
18 Poland Road, Glenfield
Auckland 10, New Zealand

Random House South Africa (Pty) Limited
PO Box 337, Bergvlei, South Africa

Random House UK Limited Reg. No. 954009
ISBN 0-7126-5902-1

Set in Bembo by
SX Composing Ltd., Rayleigh, Essex
Printed and bound in Great Britain by
Cox & Wyman Ltd, Reading, Berkshire

For Jim and Mirella, with love

# ACKNOWLEDGEMENTS

My thanks to: Paula Jacobs and Sean Marriott for their behind-the-scenes work on *Perfect Decisions*; my business partner Michael Maynard for his usual insightful suggestions; my family, who accept my constant stints at the keyboard with amused tolerance.

## ABOUT THE AUTHOR

Andrew Leigh trained as an economist, has an MA in Manpower Studies and is a Fellow of the IPM. He is the author of a number of books on management, most recently *Effective Change* (IPM); and *ACE Teams, Creating Star Performance in Business* (Butterworth Heinemann) written with his business partner Michael Maynard. With Michael Maynard he wrote *The Perfect Presentation* and *Perfect Communications* (Century).

He was a senior manager in the public sector for many years and is currently a partner in Maynard Leigh Associates, the management development and consultancy service whose clients include Allied Dunbar, The Body Shop, Ladbrokes, the Stock Exchange, Sun Life and Texas Home Care. You can contact Maynard Leigh Associates at

7 Rostrevor Mews,
London SW6 5AZ
Tel: 071-371 5288

# CONTENTS

# INTRODUCTION
## A WORD IN YOUR EAR

There's a striking science fiction story about a time traveller who visits a previous millennium and while there inadvertently kills a butterfly. On returning to his own time he finds everything subtly altered, because that apparently insignificant event triggers all sorts of tiny, but cumulatively large, effects.

Similarly, we can never be entirely sure what the full ramifications of our decisions will be. No matter how brilliantly we organize ourselves and our systems, unpredictable events will always keep happening. It is chaotic, and there is even a respected theory that says we can predict that chaos will always occur.

So although *Perfect Decisions* is a catchy title, we would probably not recognize a perfect decision if it stood up and bit us. Since we must all make decisions constantly in life, even though we cannot hope to make them perfect, some way of making them as good as possible seems a perfectly sensible ambition.

This book is, therefore, for anyone who wants to be better at decision making, without necessarily turning themselves into a management scientist.

*Perfect Decisions* is not quite what it seems. The first management book I wrote, back in the early 1980s, was on decision making, and it survived until recently when it slid quietly out of print. Curiously it was translated into Italian and is still going strong over there. So *Perfect Decisions* has good ancestry, while being entirely new in its own right.

The significant change since the early 1980s has been a much greater awareness among business people that so-called scientific management is no substitute for good leadership, for being creative at work, and for valuing people as an organization's only lasting source of competitive advantage.

There has consequently been a slight retreat from an excessive urge to quantify everything in sight at the expense of common sense. We now know, for example, that a personal computer on your desk and torrents of new information do not necessarily stimulate more informed decisions or make better managers.

While some truth remains in the claim that 'if you cannot measure it you cannot manage it', people are becoming wiser to the limitations of figures as ever more of them become available. Effective decision making remains what it always has been, a blend of skills drawing on an ever-changing backdrop of techniques and technologies.

I hope this book helps to improve some aspects of your decision making, and may your decisions always be optimal.

Andrew Leigh

# LET'S BE RATIONAL

How likely are you to be wrong? Do you think you mainly get decisions right or often make bad mistakes? Like most people, you probably feel your decisions are sound and are reasonably confident about them.

Few of us admit to lacking faith in our judgement. In a survey of British motorists, for example, nearly everyone (95 per cent) thought they were a better-than-average driver, which is clearly impossible.

The better your education, the more likely you possess an inflated opinion of your effectiveness as a decision maker. Research has repeatedly demonstrated how, for instance, doctors, engineers and financial advisers all have an unjustified belief in their judgements.

> 66 **Many of our executives make very sound decisions. The trouble is many of them have turned out not to have been right.** 99
>
> *Donald Bullock, Training Director, C&P Telephone Company*

A reason for overconfidence is that we usually prefer evidence supporting our views, rather than information that contradicts it or reduces trust in our judgement.

If you are thinking of buying a house, for example, and have already formed a highly favourable view of it, the tendency is to screen out any bad news, sometimes not even look for it. There are many instances of people moving into a new home and later expressing surprise that the roof needed replacing or the place was filled with dry rot. There was often ample evidence of these factors before signing the contract. They simply preferred not to look.

Since we cannot be certain about the consequences of a decision, important choices tend to be based on an intuitive estimate of the probabilities – that is, the chance of something happening. Research underlines that human beings are poor at calculating probabilities, whether in making bets or calculating the risks from a medical operation.

Decision making should be about making rational, sensible choices. Indeed we all like to think of ourselves as rational human beings. In practice everybody is irrational some of the time. The more complex the decision the more irrational we tend to be.

---

**66 The great decisions of human life have, as a rule, more to do with instincts and other mysterious unconscious factors than with conscious will and well-meaning reasonableness. 99**
*Carl Jung*

---

A powerful factor clouding our judgement is emotion, yet it competes with many other inherent defects in the way people think. Here are some facts you may want to consider:

- Authority figures can distort people's ability to make important decisions

Example: co-pilots have felt unable to challenge the decision of the pilot that later proved fatal

- Membership of a group tends to reduce an individual's feeling of responsibility for a particular decision

    Example: football hooliganism

- Rewards, punishments, stress and strong emotions reduce flexibility of thinking and lead to irrational behaviour

    Example: a person may stay in a well-paid job even though it is making them ill

---

**66 Everyone complains of his memory, but no one complains of his judgement. 99**

*Duc de la Rochefoucauld*

---

- When an extreme event occurs we usually believe more of the same will follow, when in fact there is a natural tendency to revert to the average

    Example: just because a share does wonderfully well this year does not mean it will do so next year; it is more likely to return to the average for all shares

- Favourable first impressions influence us most – the halo effect – and later evidence is interpreted in the light of these beliefs

    Example: handsome men and women are commonly rated higher on intelligence, athletic prowess and sense of humour than is justified by the facts

● Any decision that is publicly announced is more likely to be completed than one taken privately

   Example: to maximize your chance of stopping smoking tell everyone of your intention

● If we have to reverse a decision we usually justify it by going to extremes to magnify its bad consequences

   Example: ex-lovers tend to exaggerate the awfulness of previous partners

● People who have made a sacrifice in terms of money or time to do something tend to continue doing it even when they would be better off stopping

   Example: we persist in sitting through a bad film, or fail to sell shares that have dropped in value and have no prospects

● Once we have made a decision we are often extremely reluctant to change it, even in the face of overwhelming evidence that it is wrong

   Example: managers refuse to believe their new product is failing in the marketplace and still pour money into it

---

**66 Like all weak men he laid an exaggerated stress on not changing his mind. 99**

*W Somerset Maugham*

---

● Our natural tendency to make connections often leads us to infer causes wrongly

Example: graduates earn more on average than others, so politicians have suggested that attendance at university raises earning power. Yet there may be no such cause and effect; other reasons may fully explain this result

● Our natural wish not to be different – herd instinct – can convince us that the right decision is the one that everyone else is taking, when the exact opposite may be true

Example: when there is a major scramble out of shares it may be the best time to start buying

---

**66 Why do you have to be a nonconformist like everybody else?99**

*James Thurber*

---

● Actuarial calculations are usually more reliable than pure judgement, if we can obtain information on a sufficient number of cases on which to base decisions

Example: we may put our personal chances of getting cancer from smoking as fairly low because we like to think these things always happen to someone else, not us. Actuarial figures, though, show that the chances are quite high

These are all aspects of human behaviour in decision making that Stuart Sutherland, Professor of Psychology at Sussex University, has called irrationality. People simply do not perform in the logical way the evidence or facts would suggest they should do.

While a more scientific approach to decisions can certainly enhance many choices, the difference is often marginal. A far greater influence is what might be called applied psychology.

When we use our understanding of how people tend to behave, this can be a major help in making better decisions. For instance, while many investors use complicated methods of analysing currency movements, the most successful operators make millions – sometimes billions – through anticipating how the rest of the market will react. Their actions seldom owe much to formal decision-making techniques.

A wider meaning of rationality therefore includes a good dose of common sense, often dressed up as applied psychology, and at the margin the use of formal methods of analysis that can help make sense of some complex choices.

Since you probably cannot hope to be a paragon of rationality, however much you study psychology, follow decision rules or calculate probabilities, what does this mean for your day-to-day decision making?

In practice it implies the best action is acquiring and using knowledge about decision making to increase the chances of getting it right, and avoiding the more disastrous consequences of getting it wrong.

---

**66 In every success story you find someone has made a courageous decision.99**

*Peter Drucker, international management consultant*

---

# WHAT IS A DECISION?

Right now you face a choice. Either to continue with this book or not. A decision is simply what happens when we make up our minds, and even when we don't we are still making a decision – a decision not to decide.

We need to make decisions because we are constantly either

- Responding to change, or
- Initiating change

---

**66 Nothing endures but change. 99**

*Heraclitus*

---

Nothing remains the same in this world. Even the stars move over the centuries. In our everyday human existence we cannot rely on always behaving in the same way. Our work environment, colleagues or market forces are continually altering. Therefore we must make decisions to meet the challenges.

## DECISION NEEDED?

Three conditions must exist before we can be sure a decision is required:

- **Two or more** possible outcomes – otherwise there is no choice
- **Some value or importance** attached to these outcomes – if none is significant there is no real choice to make
- **Variations** in the effectiveness of outcomes and how much we want them – for when all are equally desirable or effective, why bother to choose?

> **66 It's easy to make good decisions – when there are no bad options. 99**
>
> **Robert Half, President, Robert Half International**

When people decide, in essence they have to ask themselves

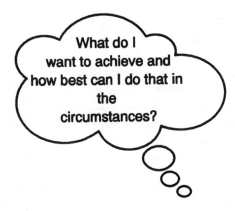

Maybe you feel it is time to improve your decision making. Perhaps someone has recommended that you should brush up on the subject. Is this the right book or even the right way? Would a short training course be better? Is this a good time or place to be reading?

All these thoughts may be whizzing through your mind yet here you are, still reading! So what has been going on?

The precise moment you make a decision is

- An Event
  The point when you decide, or decide not to choose

All the activity leading to this decision, the thoughts passing through your mind, holding the book, maybe even buying it and so on, are part of

● A Process

An important aspect of decision making is always to treat it as

● **A Process** leading to an **Event**

Since the process is a continuous sequence of activities it may be hard to break it down into discrete parts. Treating a decision solely as an isolated event can be misleading and downright unhelpful.

**All the circumstances surrounding a choice, not just the moment of choice itself, make up decision making.**

### OUTCOMES

Until we take action based on our decision, its short- and long-term effects are uncertain.

For example, suppose we believe a new do-it-yourself electric tool will help around the home. We may shop around and eventually make the purchase, happy that this gadget will now make stripping wallpaper or cutting plastic foam easier.

Once we get the box home and open it, we may discover the machine works wonders. Equally we may find it harder to use than expected and a few months later consign it to oblivion in a seldom-visited cupboard.

So each decision we make has uncertain **Outcomes** that can be good, bad or indifferent. One way of making sense of these is to produce a Payoff table. This sums up the actual or potential results of a decision.

## PAYOFF TABLE

**ACTIONS--EXPENDITURES**

|  |  | HIGH | MEDIUM | LOW |
|---|---|---|---|---|
| **CIRCUMSTANCES** | BOOM | p1 | p2 | p3 |
|  | STABLE | p4 | p5 | p6 |
|  | RECESSION | p7 | p8 | p9 |

Shows nine possible payoffs from different
levels of expenditure, under three sets of
circumstances

When we finally decide, we want to feel it is the best possible choice in the circumstances. 'Best' though may need defining. Often it amounts to choices that are 'just good enough' or ones we can justify in the face of criticism – either someone else's or our own.

Decision making deals with the impact of events in the future, which is never absolutely predictable. So a basic feature of all decision making is

• Uncertainty

Faced with choices we must ask ourselves:

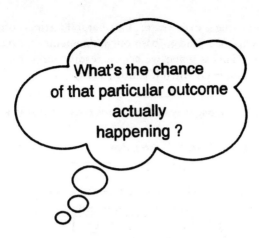

Most of the time the decisions we face are so uncertain in terms of result, we rely heavily on experience and intuition in choosing. However, there are also many situations where we can describe quite precisely the amount of uncertainty, which is

● Risk

This has a more precise meaning than uncertainty. It implies we can *quantify* the amount of uncertainty of different outcomes. Our estimates may be based on careful measurements, an intuitive, personal view of the chances of something happening, or a combination of both. This is called risk analysis (see also Chapter 6).

---

**66 Every time I took a risk I made sure that the research and marketing reports were favourable to my instincts.99**

*Lee Iacocca*

---

While the best choice may seem blindingly obvious, it may – annoyingly – turn out in practice that an entirely different one is even better. Our natural instincts often betray us. We tend to base our judgements on 'availability'. This is when we act on readily accessible information, even when it is misleading.

> 66 The wrong way always seems the more reasonable. 99
>
> **Lord Mansfield, Scottish judge**

If your friend says her or his make of car is wonderful you may decide to buy the same model. Yet it could have been a 'lucky' version and may prove more expensive to run than you expected.

Other examples of 'availability' being used to influence people's judgements are when goods are priced as £5.95 instead of £6.00; or when lottery organizers give maximum publicity to past winners while saying nothing about the losers.

Availability really means 'information that is presented'. Because it is offered to us readily, we grab at it as being immediately useful to our choice. In practice this frequently causes us to make the wrong decision.

Another case of 'availability' distorting our decision making is when we cling to existing beliefs and avoid discovering if we might be wrong. Since our beliefs are the handiest presented information, we tend to use them to make choices when other less comfortable facts could prove equally, or more, valuable.

The implications for our day-to-day choices include:

- The immediately obvious course of action is not always the best

- Do not use **only** readily available facts to make important choices
- Look behind and beyond the obvious information and apparent solutions

---

**❝ How can I believe in God when just last week I got my tongue caught in the roller of an electric typewriter?❞**

*Woody Allen*

---

## BITS VERSUS THE WHOLE

With uncertainty built into decision making it seems sensible to look at how to take it into account. One way of doing so is by reducing decision making to a series of orderly, logical stages. This approach is

- **Atomistic**

Using small steps we can concentrate fire power on the component parts and make them yield important information about

- The implications of decisions
- The reliability of information
- The need for more facts
- New alternatives or solutions
- Unsuspected causes
- Different ways of judging choices
- The timing of choices
- Ways of achieving action

By contrast, another way of handling uncertainty is to use instinct and judgement. This uses a range of intuitive methods, rather than systematic skills. This approach is

- **Holistic**

Management thinking about decision making used to veer towards either one or other of these approaches, not both. The atomistic approach was said to clash irreconcilably with the holistic one. You can see this occurring in an organization when, for example, an accountant insists the figures should govern a decision, while the marketing director claims there is more to it than just the hard financial facts.

Although the atomistic and holistic approaches are quite distinct, they converge in the most crucial activity of all

● Thinking

---

**66 You can't think rationally on an empty stomach, and a whole lot of people can't do it on a full one either.99**

*Lord Reith*

---

## PEOPLE WITH TWO BRAINS
From what we know of how the brain works there is convincing evidence that it combines these two approaches.

One reason may be because the brain is created in two linked halves. The left is said to specialize in language, sense of time and other linear functions. It deals with structure.

The right half is said to favour creative thought, intuition and the pursuit of artistic endeavours.

Both halves help us understand problems and make best guesses. It is the integration of the two approaches that enables us to be effective decision makers.

So if your personal preference is to rely mainly on facts, that's fine, but you need to be aware that making effective decisions means going further. It also involves using more uncontrollable skills like intuition and judgement to make sense of information. Facts do not necessarily 'speak for themselves'.

If your personal preference is to rely mainly on intuition, past experience, gut feeling and creative flair in making choices, that's fine too. Be aware though, many choices are counter intuitive. Having a careful look at the facts and perhaps doing some detailed analysis such as statistical calculations may help make your judgements more effective.

Throughout *Perfect Decisions* it is through combining useful ideas and approaches to making choices, not the compartmentalizing of them, that you will improve your decision making.

---

**66 If you get all the facts, your judgement can be right; if you don't get all the facts, it can't be right. 99**

*Bernard Baruch, Presidential adviser and broker*

---

## PROGRAMMED DECISIONS

Some decisions are repetitive and routine, like whether we pay our electricity bill regularly, ordering stationery or replenishing the shelves in a supermarket.

It is relatively easy to break down these types of choices into a sequence of straightforward steps.

We can decide to pay our electricity bill by direct debit. Or we can ensure stationery is automatically reordered monthly. The replacement of stock in a supermarket may be almost entirely controlled by formal decision rules.

These routine, predictable choices have increasingly been passed to computers. Programmed decisions, though, are only viable if these criteria are satisfied:

- Sufficient resources for data collection and analysis – do you have people and equipment to collect the basic facts?
- An adequate amount of quantified data – are clear records kept of previous orders, current stock, demand?
- A stable environment that won't require procedural changes at short notice – is there likely to be a sudden influx of additional staff using all the stationery?
- Sufficient skills – do any of the available people possess enough expertise to create a reliable, efficient, programmed decision process?

## UNPROGRAMMED DECISIONS

These are the opposite of programmed decisions because they are novel, unstructured and unpredictable. They rely on a more intuitive approach, dealing with situations for which there is no easily defined set of principles. They demand more emphasis on judgement, abilities and experience – the creation of 'rules of thumb' as decision aids.

Most decisions we face in life are unprogrammed and not easily dealt with by adopting a neat set of rules. This is why uncovering the elements of the decision process can be helpful in improving intuitive judgements.

**❝ No matter how deep a study you make, what you really have to rely on is your own intuition and when it comes down to it, you really don't know what is going to happen until you do it. ❞**

*Konosuke Matsushita, Founder of Matsushita Electric Co (Japan)*

## DECISION MAKERS

Research conducted some years ago suggested that top decision makers shared many important characteristics. They were self-confident and impatient to get the job done. This created a tendency to be abrupt and tactless with subordinates. When necessary they could narrow their field of vision to ignore everything but the current issue.

If you are not like this, does it mean you cannot be a good decision maker? Of course not. What is important is that these top decision makers all liked to **confront the issue directly**. They focused on essentials seeing each situation in terms of lasting effects, not problems.

Whatever our personal style we can all capitalize on our strengths to become effective decision makers at what we do.

## CHECKLIST

- Treat decision making as a process, not just an event
- A decision implies there are choices available
- Some decisions are counter intuitive
- Do not rely just on readily available facts
- Look beyond and behind the obvious information and apparent solutions

- Try defining decisions into programmed (repetitive and routine) and unprogrammed (unstructured and unpredictable)
- Recognize the role of individual values – yours and other people's – in the decision making process
- We make decisions either to respond to change, or to initiate it
- Decision making is always associated with a degree of uncertainty
- Everyone has the potential to be an effective decision maker, whatever their personal style

---

**66 No great marketing decisions have ever been made on quantitative data. 99**

*John Sculley, CEO, Apple Computer Co*

---

# THE DECISION PROCESS

> **❝ Make every decision as if you owned the whole company. ❞**
>
> *Robert Townsend, former CEO, Avis*

Could you describe the various steps you go through to make an important decision in your own personal life? See how many separate ones you can identify by writing them down.

When we list the decision steps we intend to take we are making a framework which can be shared with other people. This helps create more predictable procedures for making choices.

Company decision making in Japan tends to be highly ritualized and therefore extremely predictable. Everyone seems to understand how a choice is made and his or her role in arriving at it. The process is often about gathering consensus, even when it merely supports a senior management decision that is non-negotiable. Cynics say it is a way of ensuring no one takes personal responsibility for any important choices.

In western companies the decision process may be less clear. Yet a framework for making choices is helpful and can:

- Ensure all important steps or factors are included
- Provide a 'map' for evaluating choices and avoiding irrelevancies
- Explain our approach clearly to others
- Inspire confidence

- Document the process and justify decisions
- Allow us to analyse and set priorities quickly

Frameworks support but do not *guarantee* effective decisions. What matters is how they are used. Excessive use leads to inflexibility. They are no substitute for common sense, judgement or intuition.

---

**66 Intuition: that strange instinct that tells a woman she is right, whether she is or not. 99**
*Methodist Recorder*

---

Here is a simple five-stage decision framework:

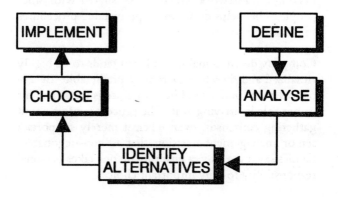

First we define the situation, its boundaries and constraints. Next we analyse the situation to make sense of it, and to unravel causes. This enables us to identify alternative courses of action or solutions, one of which we finally choose. The last step is to implement our choice.

Each of the stages needs to be carefully monitored. This lets us know what has happened at any one moment.

Some people prefer a slightly more detailed approach. For example, a study of how over 2,000 managers, supervisors and executives took decisions identified eight stages – nine if you include Monitoring.

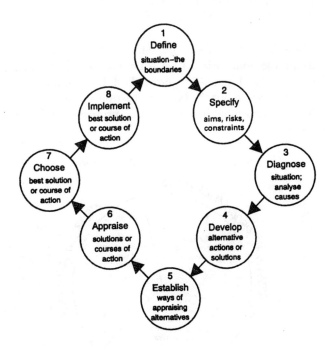

These eight stages were tested on several hundred people and most reported it helped their decision-making ability.

You would not use the framework consciously to make a simple decision such as whether to have cornflakes or muesli for breakfast. But when more complex choices are involved, it is a powerful tool for making sense of the decision process.

It may take a few tries before you become used to the framework, but you will soon find it gives your decision making a more structured approach.

1. DEFINE the situation and
2. SPECIFY the decision objectives

These first two stages in the framework are about clarifying the boundaries of the issue with which you are dealing. The Kepner-Tregoe method, for example, is a way of sorting out the type of situation you are facing by distinguishing between plans, problems and decisions.

The K–T approach: separating decisions from problems

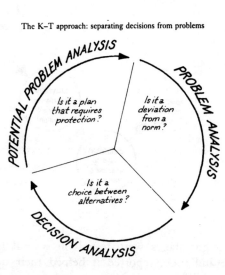

POTENTIAL PROBLEM ANALYSIS

*Is it a plan that requires protection?*

PROBLEM ANALYSIS

*Is it a deviation from a norm?*

*Is it a choice between alternatives?*

DECISION ANALYSIS

In all three types of activity, well-defined objectives – in the sense of knowing what we want – are essential.

The K–T approach treats a problem strictly as a deviation from a norm, making problem solving a more specific, analytical process. It focuses solely on finding solutions, rather than generating alternatives.

Experts are divided about how problem solving fits into decision making

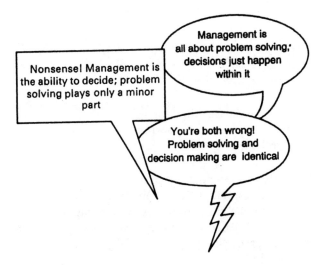

In practice there is so much overlap between problems and decisions that for most purposes it is not worth trying to make a false separation. However, you may find it helpful to use this tighter definition of a problem when you know for sure something has gone wrong and you are looking for a specific cause.

### GET CLEAR
People frequently agonize about a decision when the real issue is not choice but what you want to achieve. When you are not clear about what you want, how can you expect to make sensible decisions?

Even when people are clear about what they want, this may be an edited form of their desire rather than a full-blooded picture of their wishes. Again, this can make it hard to choose with precision.

In management jargon, we need objectives to

- Focus attention on what we want
- Minimize distractions
- Guide our intuition

Like any aspect of managing, though, we must avoid becoming fixated on a single way of working. Always demanding highly specific objectives can

- Programme the mind too narrowly
- Make us overlook opportunities
- Blind our intuition

Certainly you should adopt clear objectives, yet be willing also to respond to other opportunities and if necessary adjust the aims. Initial objectives might, for instance, be a greater return on capital, increasing market share, or producing a competitive tender.

Objectives do not stand in isolation. We should also define the associated risks and identify the constraints.

Risks need defining because they may influence our ultimate choice. We want to know the constraints because these show the limitations within which we are working.

For example, if you are thinking of buying a house at an auction you would need to assess carefully the risks of a purchase. Two constraints might be your inability to view the house before buying and to obtain a mortgage.

3.  DIAGNOSE the situation; analyse causes and
4.  DEVELOP alternatives

Here you are unravelling the situation, identifying what needs to be done or what has gone wrong. There are a multitude of techniques available to help do this, ranging from the highly technical to the inspired guess.

Eventually you need to begin generating alternatives. These may take the form of specific solutions or courses of action. Either way it involves choices.

---

66 **Guess if you can, choose if you dare.** 99

*Heraclitus*

---

Suppose the doctor says you are run down and need a holiday. You decide to go to Italy for its sun and good food. Depending on the constraints – your resources, available time and tolerance for long journeys – you might go camping or take a coach tour, have a two-week fly-drive package by the sea, or spend a week visiting art galleries.

Faced with many alternatives and possibly scores of bulging brochures, you might develop a basic list of alternatives with which to begin working.

The whole business of developing alternatives is a subject in its own right. It mixes both systematic thinking and creativity. We look at this in Chapters 5 and 6.

6.  ESTABLISH method for appraising alternatives
7.  CHOOSE best solution or course of action

During this part of the process you become clear about how you will judge the various alternatives. The method used can radically influence the final choice, so it makes sense to give this some careful thought. There are many ways of analysing and appraising alternatives. (See Chapter 5.)

The simplest approach is to select a set of criteria and check the alternatives against each of these. So, for example, you might use six criteria for choosing your Italian holiday:

| By the Sea | Cost under £500 |
| Mid-week travel | Children go free |
| Golf course nearby | Scuba diving facilities |

If you are a keen diver, scuba facilities might be far more important to you than, say, mid-week travel. So a further refinement in your method of appraisal could be to give twice as much weight to this criteria as to any other.

A company making a major investment decision may use a whole raft of criteria for selecting a specific course of action. It too might decide to weight some more heavily than others. It may even need a computer to calculate which choice emerges with the highest score.

There are many methods for making sense of alternatives, ranging from a simple list of the pros and cons, to sophisticated computer programmes that use probability and other techniques to assess choices.

Having weighed up the different alternatives the next step is making the choice. This is the point in the decision process that most people think of as decision making. As we have seen, though, this is only one step along the way, an event.

The more thoroughly the earlier stages have been performed, the easier it usually becomes to make the final decision. Thoroughness does **not** mean you have all the information necessary to make the best choice. Or that the objectives are all crystal clear and quantified. Often choices must be made on limited data and using oversimplified criteria for appraising alternatives.

Systematically undertaking each of the above stages can provide more confidence about the final choice. Ultimately, it is about using judgement, even when a computer apparently decides as, for instance, with certain schemes for buying and selling shares. Somebody had to decide the rules for the computer to use in the first place.

8.  IMPLEMENT best solution or course of action

The final stage in the decision framework is taking action of some kind, based on the choice that has been made. This may involve no action at all, but that too becomes a decision.

Implementation is the Achilles heel of many companies. While great effort goes into the earlier stages of the decision process it is often assumed that *executing* the decision will happen fairly easily. In practice it usually requires even more thoroughness and follow through.

When we implement a decision we also want to know if it has produced the result we wanted. This is a hidden, ninth stage of the framework which is not shown in the chart. It involves checking on what is happening, often called

●   MONITORING

Monitoring needs to happen throughout the decision

process, not just at the end when we are implementing a choice. So, if you wish, in the middle of the chart on page 21 you could put the single word MONITOR to indicate it must happen continuously.

## CHECKLIST

- Frameworks let us share the decision process with others
- Frameworks do not guarantee good decisions
- Consider using a simple framework
- Objectives: focus attention on what we want; minimize distractions; guide our intuition
- Define the risks and identify the constraints
- The method of appraising alternatives can radically affect the final outcome
- The more thoroughly the earlier stages of a decision are conducted, the easier it generally becomes to make the final choice
- Monitoring needs to happen throughout the decision process, not just at the implementation stage

---

**66 I like fast decisions. 99**

*Helena Rubenstein*

---

# STYLE AND INTUITION

**66 I'll give you a definite maybe. 99**

*Sam Goldwyn, film producer*

Personality and style play a big part in decision making. This is not always fully accepted; instead, there is often a smoke screen of claims about the importance of rational decision making and so on.

In business the 'rational' approach is strongly favoured at the expense of feelings or instinct. This explains why many managers remain weak in decision making.

Closely following an objective, logical approach may kill intuition and creativity. It may also breed frustration about the decision process itself.

Successful decision making means being reasoned and systematic, while still feeling free to use our 'gut' instincts:

● Use intuition creatively, don't minimize or eliminate it

## MANAGEMENT STYLE

**66 Style is knowing who you are, what you want to say, and not giving a damn. 99**

*Gore Vidal, US writer*

Endless studies on style have delved into which type works best and who tends to use which kind. The results are not inspiring. It turns out that the best management style is the one most appropriate to the situation! Thanks a lot, you may say; that will certainly not make life any easier.

The simplest style check is how far you lean towards being either systematic or intuitive. It is only by combining the two styles that you gain access to your full thinking power.

Again, there is no 'right' style except in response to a particular situation.

## SYSTEMATIC APPROACH
A systematic approach would be one where you

- Use a clear set of steps to make choices
- Are aware of both process and method
- Justify solutions by your methods
- Define constraints early in the process
- Discard alternatives after careful consideration
- Keep refining the decision situation
- Search systematically for extra information

## INTUITIVE APPROACH
An intuitive approach would be one in which you

- Keep in mind the overall decision situation, avoiding excessive focus on specifics
- Continuously redefine the problem or decision
- Justify a decision by the results
- Simultaneously consider various alternatives and options
- Jump from one step to another in the analysis, then back again
- Explore and drop alternatives quickly

## Using intuition

---

**66 I act on instinct, quickly, without pondering possible disaster and without indulging in deep introspection. 99**

*Estée Lauder*

---

Nobody is quite sure how intuition works. Perhaps it makes a direct link to subconscious stores of data in the brain. Anyway, we cannot expect it to work exactly to order. Its role has therefore seldom been fully accepted by those keen on a more systematic approach.

The intuitive approach can produce fresh or creative perspectives when we need to review choices or solutions. Being a skilled decision maker means

● Bringing fresh insights into the systematic process

It is wasteful not to use intuition. Equally, because business and management is an inexact science, it is occasionally tempting to feel that *only* instinct can provide a viable solution.

How much weight you give it depends on your style, which is

● The balance achieved between being systematic and intuitive

There are also hidden forces affecting decision making, like

● Fear – we may become overcautious and unwilling to pursue new or creative alternatives
● Self-interest – we may make choices that seem

better for us than they really are

- Personality clashes – we may discount other people's input or reject their opinions through taking a dislike to them personally

## INDECISIVENESS

> 66 There is no more miserable human being than one in whom nothing is habitual but indecision. 99
>
> *William James, American professor of psychology*

Are you a ditherer? At times we may all be terribly undecided and it may not matter a bit. If you vacillate over whether to have tea or coffee, so what? Real indecisiveness is when we face **important** choices and either delay too long in making one or avoid it altogether.

Most managers see themselves as decisive, priding themselves on their bias for action. Yet those in positions of authority are sometimes too precipitous when more reflection would be better. Sadly, reflection is often equated with being indecisive.

There are also real obstacles to being decisive. Stress, for instance (See Chapter 7), can cause indecision, as can

- Fear of repeating past mistakes
- Too much or too little information
- Too much consultation
- Uncertainty
- Role confusion
- Inertia
- Time pressures
- Fear of the effect of our action

> 66 **Decisiveness is often the art of timely cruelty.** 99
>
> *Henri Becque, French playwright*

## Fear of past mistakes

Past blunders can seriously deter decision making. This is particularly true in large, hierarchical organizations that create ways to minimize the chance of decision error. The methods include committees, groups of experts and formalized decision procedures.

While meant to help, such devices may create anxiety about the penalties for mistakes. Understandably, people react by making fewer decisions and taking fewer risks.

> 66 **Well, if I called the wrong number, why did you answer the phone?** 99
>
> *James Thurber*

## Available information

Are you an info freak? These are master ditherers who keep demanding facts to avoid making a decision. They only feel comfortable with information overkill. The latter causes indigestion in the decision process.

In their zeal for more data info freaks stifle intuition. It is hard to develop creative solutions or imaginative alternatives when faced with demands for a bottomless pit of so-called 'facts'.

The amount of available information for decisions is often

- Too little – yet a choice must still be made
- Too much – with insufficient time or skill to use it

What we use and how we interpret it is prone to bias. Statistical evidence, in particular, has an air of impartial authority it rarely deserves. To make the best of information and avoid being an info freak, keep asking yourself

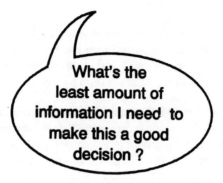

What's the least amount of information I need to make this a good decision ?

**Risk**
How much uncertainty we can stand depends on our personality and experience.

• All decisions involve some uncertainty and risk

By refusing to confront risk we may indirectly promote indecisiveness, overreliance on information or excessive consultation.

> **66 The entire contents of the policy manual of the $1.9 billion Nordstrom Corporation: 'Use your own judgement at all times.'99**

Sometimes the amount of risk can be quantified. While attaching probabilities to some events gives a spurious air of accuracy to our choices, proper risk analysis can

- Clarify choices
- Show which choices are undesirable
- Prompt informed debate
- Reveal what information is needed
- Increase the chance of making a decision

## Consultation

Former Prime Minister Margaret Thatcher's approach to consultation was said by critics to be: 'I listen to what you have to say, we all argue about it for a while, then we do as I say.'

This approach is rather extreme, yet it remains true that a decision may be hard to obtain if too many people are involved. This happens because of

- A too hierarchical structure
- An overrigid framework of procedures
- Decision makers unsure of their own judgement
- A need to share the blame for mistakes
- Confusion between consultation and participation

We particularly need to distinguish between **consultation** and **participation**. In the latter, people help make the actual decision. With consultation people are asked for their views but do not necessarily make the final decision.

Managers frequently send confusing messages about their wish to involve people. This can slow down the whole decision process until the question of how people can contribute is expanded.

The main ways of involving other people in your decision making are shown on the next page.

I've made my decision, take it or leave it

## TELLING

This is my decision, let me tell you about it, and try to convince you it's a good one

## SELLING

This is what I'd like to do. What do you think about it?

## PRESENTING

I'm thinking of this possible action. How would you improve it?

## CONSIDERING

Here's the problem. Let's have your ideas and I can base my decision on your contributions

## CONSULTING

Here's the full situation and various constraints we face. Let's try to make the final decision together

## PARTICIPATING

You're responsible and you know what you're doing. I trust you to make the decision

## DELEGATING

There is a sound case for favouring consultation and delegation in much of today's company decision making. For example, it helps enrol people in the decision.

Much depends though on how you organize people's involvement. We need to judge the right approach in each case, not use one inflexible rule.

### Role confusion

Uncertainty about what is required, and by whom, explains why many decisions are delayed or never made. To improve your decision making and prevent some choices from being overlooked

• Establish people's actual responsibilities

When you clarify duties there is less chance of each person assuming someone else is making the decision.

### Inertia

When there are elaborate checks or procedures to minimize risk, you can become isolated from reality. The same can happen if you overdelegate without also giving away the power to make the final decision.

Formal procedures are meant to free people in their decision making. In practice, if not used wisely these can obstruct initiative, promote passivity and encourage inertia. Excess delegation may also leave a formal decision maker unable to do more than ratify a proposed decision or delay it. The latter may be the only way to demonstrate personal authority.

Equally, it seems easier to make decisions in response to a challenge of some kind, rather than taking an initiative. We tend to avoid choices until we are forced to make them.

- Good delegation means handing over the power to make a decision
- Excess delegation leaves a formal decision maker only able to delay action
- Be active in identifying new choices to be made

**Time pressures**

Does lack of time seem to make systematic decision making impossible? That is certainly how many people see it. While time is certainly an important constraint, it is how you are organized to make the best use of it that most affects the decision.

Too much time can be harmful. For example, there is evidence that too many managers suffer a paralysis of analysis. Time pressures are an essential ingredient of decision making. So to make better choices

- Take control of your time

When you are well organized you will feel more able to be decisive. Are there ways of giving yourself more time for the various decision processes? For example, can you break down decisions into a series of smaller, more manageable choices?

Perhaps you can delegate parts of the decision process. Someone else might become responsible for gathering information, arranging an appraisal method, or generating alternatives.

---

66 **All decisions should be made as low as possible in the organization. The Charge of the Light Brigade was ordered by an officer who wasn't there looking at the territory.** 99

*Robert Townsend, former CEO, Avis*

---

## CHECKLIST

- Use your personality; don't force it out of sight when making choices, because there's no perfect management style for decision making
- Respond appropriately to situations rather than adopting the same approach to everything
- Be aware of your intuition; learn when to rely on it and when to look for harder information on which to base choices.
- Recognize the obstacles to decision making and practise overcoming them
- Be discriminating in your use of facts
- Do not expect to have complete information to make most decisions
- Take control of your time through planning, organization and delegation
- Break complex decisions into smaller, simpler parts; don't be afraid to delegate parts of the decision process
- When involving others in the process, be explicit about their roles

---

**66 Half the pictures are never made, because the partners don't have the guts to say to each other, 'Let's do it!'99**

*Michael Powell, film director*

---

# TOOLS OF THE TRADE

> 66 **Whenever decisions are made strictly on the basis of bottom-line arithmetic, human beings get crunched along with the numbers. 99**
>
> *Thomas Horton, President and CEO, American Management Association*

**Decision Analysis** is the catch-all title of a large kit bag of techniques that rely on quantification for their success. The methods

- Solve complex problems
- Systematically evaluate alternatives
- Make predictions
- Bring a scientific approach to making choices

It all works on the principle of 'divide and conquer'. This reflects our tendency to solve problems by first breaking them into their component parts and dealing with each in turn.

One of the most widely used decision analysis tools is simply a sheet of paper divided in half lengthwise. On one side you list the pros of a choice and on the other the cons. Not only does this work well, it is easy to use.

After listing the pros and cons you might go further and estimate how much importance to attach to each one. The American statesman Benjamin Franklin first wrote about this aid to making choices in 1772. Where he found a pro and a con equal in importance he cancelled them both out. If one pro equalled two cons he cancelled out all three. If he found two pros equalled three cons he cancelled these out and so on.

Eventually Franklin found he was left with only a few pros and cons and could apply his judgement more easily.

What Franklin was doing was using an early form of weighting, which has since taken on some wondrous forms based on applied statistics.

Decision analysis usually forces greater clarity about

- Who are the decision makers?
- What weight will each person have in making the decision?
- What are the various alternatives to be considered?
- What criteria will be used for appraising the alternatives?
- What weight will be given to each criterion?
- How will the various criteria be applied?
- What are the chances of this result happening?
- What might stop this outcome from happening?

## DECISION MAKERS

Where several people are supposed to be taking part in a decision, it is often assumed that everyone will have the same influence on the final choice. Reality may suggest otherwise. For example, will the managing director have the final word, or is his or her influence twice or three times that of anyone else in the team?

Decision analysis can improve the rationality of the process by defining exactly how much weight each person will have in making the final decision.

### Advantages

The advantages of decision analysis include:

- The problem is defined explicitly
- A series of logical steps is used
- Subjective and objective factors are employed
- The search for data is limited
- Experts from other areas can contribute their views
- The process is documented
- A decision is communicated through quantified and written data

## Disadvantages
The drawbacks are:

- It is time-consuming and usually unsuited to quick decisions
- Assessing probabilities is subjective and may be unacceptable
- Areas where data cannot be quantified easily may be ignored
- People must cooperate to make it effective

Unless you intend to become an expert in this field the best action you can take is:

- Be willing to consult specialists where appropriate
- Be aware of what is available
- Learn to use a few tools well

## USING EXPERTS
Accountants, lawyers and market researchers are well established in business. However, there are others – like economists, statisticians, operational researchers and actuaries – who can help improve certain decisions.

What such experts have in common is an understanding of probability, mathematical model building and statistical techniques. Their disciplines can bring precision to the process of choosing.

> 66 How could I have been so far off base? All my life
> I've known better than to depend on the experts.
> How could I have been so stupid, to let them go
> ahead?99
>
> *John F. Kennedy, after the Bay of Pigs fiasco*

Using expert advice for decisions may be necessary but it can be fraught with difficulty. For example, the history of decisions to buy computer systems is riddled with financial and technical disasters. Despite a bevy of experts, and experts monitoring the experts, the Stock Exchange's Taurus settlement system was abandoned at a cost of millions of pounds.

- Choose your experts with care
- Use decision experts only when the stakes are high
- Check whether the decision process will really gain from adding expert know-how

## AWARENESS

It is unnecessary to learn *all* the many decision aids that have been developed. For most managers it is enough to become aware of what is available and be familiar with a few to be used regularly. The tools available include:

- Statistical methods
- Information systems
- Decision models
- Linear programming
- Decision trees
- Network analysis
- Marginal analysis
- Cost-effectiveness analysis
- Utility theory
- Heuristics

**43**

Do not confuse these tools with decision making itself. At best they make a slight contribution to an effective decision compared with more powerful factors like common sense and applied psychology.

The key to using a decision tool well is understanding

- WHICH tool to select
- WHEN to use it
- HOW to use it

## ADOPT A FEW TOOLS

Some personal effort is needed to apply decision analysis. Even the decision framework in Chapter 2 must be used several times before you can expect to see an improvement in the quality of decision making.

Learn a few tools and how to apply them properly, rather than attempt to master many and use none well. Badly applied decision tools do more harm than good.

For example, if you feel basic probability distributions might help, make sure you really understand what they do, how to apply them and their limitations. This applies even if you employ an expert to do the number crunching.

### Statistical methods

---

**66 I could prove God statistically. 99**

*George Gallup, American pollster*

---

Statistics have a rather dubious reputation, and with some justification. We all know how public opinion polls, for example, can be absolutely wrong. Newspapers constantly report surveys without explaining their reliability, sampling size or limitations.

Despite these image problems, statistics are a manager's best friend. They are obedient, easily trained and work doggedly to provide what is required.

Used properly, statistics provide the evidence on which to make hard choices. Decisions such as whether to launch a new product, reduce labour costs, or which machine to phase out may all depend on detailed analysis using a range of statistical tools.

These days, competent managers are expected to have a working knowledge of applied statistics including

- Averages and dispersion
- Indices
- Time series
- Sampling
- Regression
- Probability and probability distributions

Surprisingly, even big companies neglect some of the simplest methods, such as using different kinds of averages.

Statistical methods can

- Help unravel cause and effect
- Predict trends
- Show links between one variable and another

The careful accumulation of numerical data may meet obstacles such as

- Cost
- Time
- Complexity
- Difficulty

These help to explain a notable reluctance by some managers to move away from intuitive methods.

---

**66 Facts speak louder than statistics. 99**

*Geoffrey Streatfield, lawyer*

---

### Probability

Probability gives a precise meaning to 'chance'. It deals with risk as a **measurable factor**. Statisticians talk of probability as the **likelihood** that something will or will not happen and use two distinct ideas.

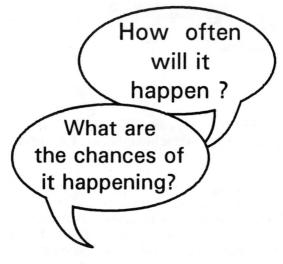

How often something happens can sometimes be precisely calculated and decisions based on the result. The likelihood of your home being burgled in the next 12 months, for instance, is based on information such as geographical location, size of premises and so on.

Using these facts an insurance company calculates the chances of a break-in. Thus your premium is based on hard evidence – objective probabilities.

In business, probabilities can be attached to all sorts of activities. For example, companies have assessed the likelihood of competitors raising their prices, exchange rates altering, circuits failing, the delivery of raw materials on time, faulty workmanship, and defective goods.

Medicine, engineering and manufacturing are all areas where probability can make a significant difference to decisions. It is worth using when

- You can collect many cases of an occurrence
- Personal estimates on probabilities are considered usable
- The importance of the decision justifies the cost of analysis

Personal estimates of probability are highly subjective and therefore suspect. Nevertheless, even opinions can be combined to give a more quantified idea about possible outcomes.

For instance, experts might give their views on the likelihood of future events, as in the Delphi Technique. This takes experts' views and after combining them feeds them back to these same experts who then adjust their views based on the new information. The final combined views produce a picture of the likelihood of how the future will look.

Probabilities are difficult to understand and require a good feel for logic. There are now easy-to-use, PC-based computer systems for applying probabilities. Crystal Ball from the Roderick Manhattan Group, for instance, should give professional statisticians a sense of job insecurity. It works within a spreadsheet and makes risk assessment and using probabilities simple.

## Information management systems

---

**66 Facts are power. 99**
*Harold Geneen, former CEO, IT&T*

---

Facts are the currency of decision making. With complete information there would be no uncertainty and hence no real choice.

This seldom, if ever, happens. So we must develop skills in obtaining, analysing and evaluating relevant data. Management information systems, for instance, have been developed to improve these tasks.

There are many information systems available that aim to assist decision makers. These are usually computer based and help define, collect, sort and summarize the facts. They are a mixture of databases, spreadsheets and executive aids.

Using them, though, can lead to an explosion of yet more information, posing as many problems as it solves.

Therefore we must be able to identify our need for facts precisely enough to obtain something useful. Effective information should be

- Timely – is it up to date and available when we need it?
- Relevant – does it have a specific bearing on the matter in hand?
- Available – can we obtain access to it?
- Intelligible – do we understand its true meaning?
- Manageable – can we handle it effectively, so it becomes useful?
- Obtainable economically

The test of usefulness of a system is whether it enhances the decision process or merely makes it more complex, difficult to control and hard to understand.

---

**66 The trouble with facts is that there are so many of them. 99**

*Samuel McChord Crothers in The Gentle Reader*

---

### Decision models

If you learn to fly a jumbo or a fighter plane you spend part of your training in a simulated aircraft that never leaves the ground. It is like a giant video game, with all the elements of a live aircraft, from real instrument panels to moving pictures of the ground.

Models to help with decision making do not use tangible equipment like aircraft simulators. Instead, mathematical tools using probabilities and variables simulate different decision situations, outcomes and payoffs.

If you are someone who uses a computer spreadsheet, you may already be using a model. For instance, when you alter variables in a business plan to see what effect this has on profits or costs.

Models help us understand the choices before finally making a decision such as

- The optimal size of an order
- Whether to accept a discount for large orders
- The best reordering level for an article of stock
- Whether to invest
- Which market to enter
- Pricing tactics
- Corporate strategy

To be effective models need

- A quantified statement of what is to be achieved
- A knowledge of the constraints under which the model will operate
- A defined set of variables and how they interrelate

Generating the list of variables to include in the model along with the probabilities, then building them into a mathematical formula to represent the live situation, is a skilled task.

While not all decision models need be complex, they *do* demand mathematical facility.

---

**66 I never could make out what those damned dots meant. 99**

*Lord Randolph Churchill on decimal points*

---

### Linear Programming

Linear programming is an advanced statistical tech-nique and a separate decision tool in its own right. It helps find the best result, such as maximum profit or minimum cost when the factors involved are subject to some constraint. For example, there may be only 1,000 hours of labour available or so many days to launch a product.

Linear programming can help when

- The situation can be stated in numerical terms
- All factors in the situation have a linear relationship – for example, doubling output requires double the labour force
- There are restrictions on the factors involved

The main drawback of linear programming is that many of the relationships encountered in decision making are not linear. For instance, by doubling wages we may not necessarily obtain twice as much output.

### Decision tress

Decision trees are a visual way of explaining choices and outcomes, forcing you to think in a structured, controlled way. To devise one we might look at

- Alternatives – what can be done?
- Consequences – what could happen?
- Desirability of outcome – how much do we want what could happen?
- Probability of outcome – how likely is it to happen?

An example that links these elements is shown on the next page. The 'Highs' and Lows' would need to be given some subjective, numerical scores.

## DECISION TREE--MY CAREER

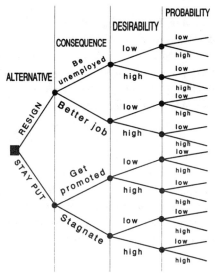

To evaluate the outcomes we would multiply the desirability score by the probability score in each case. We would then compare the total scores across the various alternatives. The one with the highest score would be the favoured choice.

The attractions of the decision tree include

- Ease of use
- Suitable for enhancement by computer

### Networks
Networks are not exotic toys straight from business school but highly practical ways of controlling projects. They help with the planning, organizing and management of tasks and resources. There is always a defined objective, usually with constraints on time and cost.

The two kinds of networks often used to improve decision making are:

- Project Evaluation and Resource Tracking (PERT)
- Critical Path Analysis (CPA)

These were originally developed to control complex projects, such as building a space rocket or constructing a motorway. **All** the project's activities are listed along with how long each will take and what resources, such as labour hours, material costs and so on it requires.

A chart is drawn showing the sequence of events and how each activity is linked. For example, to make a cup of tea, which is it best to do first: boil the water, get out the cups and saucers, or find the sugar and milk? The critical path is the essential and shortest route to completing the project.

Networks allow you to control

- Tasks
- Resources
- Costs
- Time

With this information you can decide

- The order in which each activity should occur
- The fastest route to completing a project
- Slack time in the system
- Optimal use of resources
- Which activities might run in parallel
- How deadlines alter if activities are not completed on time
- How best to respond if an activity is running late or ahead of time

There are now some excellent and easy-to-use computer aids for creating networks. Microsoft Project and CA SuperProject are both programs that work on a PC and can be used by the average manager with no previous experience of networking. Such programs will

- Draw various sorts of charts
- Develop a network to show the complete project
- Calculate the critical path
- Track the various resource implications

### Marginal analysis

This comes from the field of economics and is a way of making sense of decisions such as 'How much extra profit will we make if we increase our output?' It takes a harsh and strictly numerical look at comparing additional revenues with additional costs.

As you might expect, marginal analysis works on the margin. It quantifies what the cost of producing one extra unit would be and the resulting profit. It can be used to decide the maximum efficiency of a machine. In other words, it can find the point at which a machine's increased productivity is outweighed by increased running and maintenance costs.

Marginal analysis really puts decision makers on the spot. By nailing down the precise cost and gain from an extra unit of output it forces clarity about how to attribute overheads and other costs that often confuse the true state of affairs.

Marginal analysis tends to remain the territory of economists and, to a lesser extent, informed accountants.

### Cost-effective analysis

This technique helps with choosing the best plan when the objectives are less specific than sales, costs or profits. It ascribes costs to intangibles such as good public relations, employee morale and so on, and links them to their effect on profits. It then aims for the best ratio of benefits and costs.

It is sometimes also called cost benefit analysis. It has been used to assess, for instance, the environmental impact of a project, and to place a value on human injuries that would be awarded government compensation.

### Utility Theory

Utility Theory shows how best to achieve one's goals. It uses a measure of the DESIRABILITY (or lack of it) to an individual of different outcomes.

By adding up the desirability of all the outcomes to all the individuals and linking them with the chance of them happening, a picture is created of the most favoured course of action. Utility Theory

- Helps people overcome their own irrationality
- Forces less acceptable evidence to be used
- Sets a standard for rational decision making
- Takes full account of desires and maximizes them

Its drawbacks include the difficulty of getting people to

- Estimate their preferences correctly and assign consistent values to outcomes.
- Understand the nature of Utility Theory and how it works

### Heuristics

Heuristics looks at the link between human problem solving and artificial intelligence. It is an educational process that allows learning to happen through experience. A heuristic program has facilities for the computer to 'learn' as it proceeds, by trial and error.

By looking at how we process information and solve problems, and relating this to computer technology, we can improve our ability to make unprogrammed decisions.

### CHECKLIST

- Become aware of the main decision tools
- Learn a few decision tools well
- Decision-making tools are not a substitute for decision making itself
- The key to successful decision making is choosing WHICH tool to use and knowing HOW to use it
- Consider using decision analysis to evaluate alternatives systematically

- Be aware of obstacles to decision-making tools: doubts about their effectiveness, lack of familiarity with their potential, and other limitations within decision makers themselves

---

**66 As far as the laws of mathematics refer to reality, they are not certain; and as far as they are certain, they do not refer to reality. 99**

*Albert Einstein*

---

# GROUP DECISION MAKING

## WHY GROUPS?

> 66 In individuals, insecurity is rare; but in groups, parties, nations and epochs it is the rule. 99
>
> *Nietzche*

Human beings need each other; most of us have always lived in groups. Some companies, like hi-tech Sun Microsystems, work entirely through groups, arguing that this is why they have been so successful.

Even when groups do not make the decision, they are often the key influence on the final choice.

To improve your own decision making you need to know

- What groups can contribute
- The drawbacks of groups
- How to get the best from groups

We have seen earlier, in Chapter 2, how decision making is a process rather than a single event. Even when the actual decision is best taken by a single person, a group can be a powerful support throughout.

Groups can be useful to help evaluate the different choices and arrive at some broad conclusions.

## GROUP BENEFITS
There are occasions when groups are not helpful, for

example, when too many people are involved, leading to delays and confusion. Use a group approach when

- There are several potentially workable solutions
- Solutions may be difficult to assess objectively
- The problem or decision has many steps or sub-divisions
- A large amount of data is needed to make an informed choice
- Others need to be convinced of the decision's validity
- There are interested parties to consult to ensure implementation
- The group needs to own the decision

Groups can improve the decision process because they

- Handle variety well
- Save time
- Offer knowledge
- Reduce bias
- Overcome resistance
- Organize the task

### Variety
Groups usually produce more variety of approaches to a decision or problem than the same number of individuals working alone.

While a group is not *always* more creative than an individual working alone, that is often the result.

Groups also allow people to exchange views and by combining these create yet more possibilities. This is

- SYNERGY

The whole is greater than the sum of the parts

For decision making, synergy means more of a creative approach, using everyone's contribution.

## Time

Secondly, groups can usually invest more working time on a decision than the same number of individuals. The high cost of the group may be offset by the benefits of having the resources for making a high-quality decision.

A decision that requires an input from several people can happen more quickly in a group. Instead of being consulted individually, they can all be brought together and take part in the decision process. This also allows them to discuss and better understand their role in it. Groups, though, tend to be slow decision takers.

---

**66 We can't have a crisis next week. My diary is already full. 99**

*Henry Kissinger*

---

## Knowledge

As organizations grow it becomes harder for an individual to make important decisions in isolation. Specialized areas demand a greater breadth of both skills and knowledge.

A group will possess better total knowledge and skills than any one member. It has access to better information.

## Bias

Groups can successfully reduce or anticipate the effects of prejudice.

Confrontation and discussion help us see our beliefs for what they are – often based on the flimsiest of premises.

When they are not discussed or analysed they remain in our minds as fundamental truths.

Groups can promote objectivity, for example the jury system in criminal trials.

### Overcoming resistance
Groups are a valuable way of overcoming resistance to new ideas. Involving key people in the early stages creates more understanding about choices.

It also enrols them in finding and carrying out workable solutions.

### Communication
Group situations can free up the flow of ideas and opinions. By discussing mutual preferences a better understanding can be reached about the decision and its likely effects.

### Organization
Groups that must reach consensus tend to organize the task more than individuals. The various parts of the decision process can be subdivided so that the job as a whole becomes more ordered.

Joint work leads to improved choices and a better decision process.

### THE DOWNSIDE
The drawbacks of using a group include

- Activity overlap
- Conformity
- Risk taking
- Social forces

- Status considerations
- Expert power
- Personality and vested interests

## Activity overlap

This occurs where a group breaks down complex issues into many individual tasks which are allocated to group members. This lets people focus on a specialized area best suited to their experience or abilities.

However, this can just as readily cause people to lose sight of the broader task. The result can leave most people highly knowledgeable about only one aspect of the decision situation and unable to let go of their views in the greater interest of the wider task. A way to prevent this is to stop people concentrating only on their specialist area.

## Conformity

> 66 Conformity is the jailer of freedom and the enemy of growth. 99
>
> *John F. Kennedy*

Groups tend to promote uniformity. Social pressures can force people to go along with the group against their own inner beliefs. While this can be helpful in getting people to work together it is dangerous to effective decision making.

Conformity restricts the full consideration of alternatives. One well-known effect is group think. This is when nearly everyone in the group wants a proposed course of action so there is great pressure not to consider any alternative or opposition to what the group desires.

Faced with a decision in a committee, people sometimes say, 'This is setting a precedent.' Such a response is not merely conformist, it is irrational. If the creation of a precedent means there will be a sensible decision then this is a good precedent. If it is not a sensible decision it would be a bad precedent.

A way of countering overconformity and group think is to have two or more groups tackling the issue. Bringing them together in a 'shoot out' then reveals the important differences that either group may have missed.

### Risk taking
A common belief is that groups are overcautious and unadventurous. Research has shown the opposite is true.

Groups tend to be higher risk takers than their members acting separately. Group attitudes tend to be more extreme. This needs to be considered when setting a brief and assessing any proposals.

Proper discussion of likely outcomes may allay people's fears about the risks involved. More pragmatically, with a group decision the apportionment of blame is spread more widely. One way of dealing with this is to make the group responsible both for making the decision and carrying it out.

### Status considerations
Groups are usually less effective if there is competition for the leadership. With a senior authority figure in the group there is a danger that more time will be spent discussing, accepting or rejecting *their* views than looking for alternatives.

Asking the group to appoint its own leader with an agreed date to review the role may help.

### Expert power

The presence of an expert creates similar problems to having a formal authority figure as leader. Other group members may lack sufficient specialized knowledge to contradict the expert's views and can feel forced to agree without question.

Undue deference inhibits new approaches to problem solving and looking at new alternatives. The solution is to keep the experts on tap, not on top.

### Personality and vested interests

Even without formal power, strong personalities may damage a group's performance. If they are charismatic or domineering their input may carry excessive weight.

They may also have their own agenda that is incompatible with the general aims of the group. Some people may even adopt a stance merely to win an argument.

A decision-making group needs to be reasonably balanced in terms of its personalities.

### MAKING GROUPS EFFECTIVE

Factors causing a group to be an effective decision maker include

- Clear aims
- Commitment
- Size
- Understanding the decision process
- Matching the group to the task

### Aims

Groups often struggle with decision making because they are unsure of their remit. It pays to get this right through a rigorous statement of what is expected and by when.

## Commitment

Without commitment from all the members, the group will not tackle the decision process with its full energy. Two ways of encouraging commitment are

- Letting people volunteer for membership
- Allowing the group a major part in defining its aims

## Size

There is no ideal size of group for decision making. The optimum size of a top management team, though, is usually five or six people. An uneven number can prevent deadlock.

Small groups tend to be cohesive. This encourages people to cooperate and be more committed to reaching agreement. They also provide scope for everyone to make a contribution. Out of necessity the more reticent members are encouraged to participate.

Attitudes in large groups tend to be more dogmatic than in smaller ones. With a large audience, status-conscious participants may feel they have more to protect.

It is also harder to back down in a large group. This can lead to people taking fixed positions and seeking to protect their reputation rather than finding the best solution.

## Understanding the decision process

A group should understand the decision process it is using. Otherwise there is likely to be confusion at some point in its work. When the decision process is uncertain, more time is spent arguing about what is supposed to happen next than doing the actual work needed.

Knowledge of the decision process is different from having clear aims. In setting the aims, though, the process for making choices may need to be explained.

- Try to ensure that any group you are involved with knows the basic steps it will use for making decisions.

### Matching group to task
What needs to be done – the group task – should be the main factor in selecting both the members of the group and methods employed. Too many project groups begin life with the handicap of having the wrong people or adopting inappropriate methods.

When you have a free hand to decide who should be in a group, it is not always easy to predict exactly how those chosen will interact. Aim to create a climate where uninhibited relations allow the group to look at uncomfortable choices without flinching.

It may not be essential for all the members of the group to like each other in order to solve a problem or make a decision. However, it it usually desirable that they can get on with each other and show mutual respect. Otherwise, too much energy may go into dealing with egos and not enough on the decision.

Examples of where matching the group to the task may be advisable include:

- ROUTINE DECISION MAKING: Using specialists whose efforts require coordination. Responsibilities in the group should be decentralized to prevent one person taking control.
- NEGOTIATION: Various interested parties may be involved under the guidance of an impartial

chairperson. The main thrust of the chair role should be to obtain a decision, not to pursue a personal agenda.

- CREATIVE DECISION MAKING: This may demand the generation of many ideas and their eventual reduction to a hard core on which decisions will be made.

How the group is helped to be creative is also important. It may be better to use someone from outside the group itself to promote an effective process.

## CHECKLIST

- Recognize that groups are an important and unavoidable part of organizational decision making
- Know the pros and cons of using groups, particularly
     What groups contribute to decision making
     The drawbacks of groups in the decision process
     How to get the best from groups
- Use group decision making as a way of generating commitment
- Make sure the decision-making group has clear aims and understands the decision process
- Try to match the group to the task
- Encourage participation from all members of the group
- Try to create smaller groups where possible, as they tend to be more cohesive

# STRESS

**66 I don't have ulcers, I give them. 99**
*Harry Cohen, US film producer*

You can hardly read a magazine or watch television without seeing some health warning about stress. Along with the perils of an unhealthy diet, it is now widely seen as a major contributor to making us vulnerable to illness – from colds to back pain, from cancer to heart disease.

Less is said about another major victim of stress – our judgement. Any serious emotional state can do terrible damage to our ability to make sound judgements – as the number of marriages that end in divorce seem to confirm.

Emotion may be hard to control, but for effective decisions it is essential to know when your judgement might be becoming unduly clouded by strong feelings. The effects of stress can surface just when important decisions are being made and consequently distort judgement. The pressure to make decisions may itself cause stress.

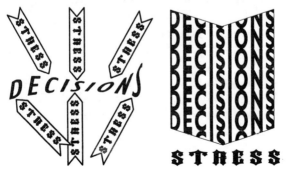

To some extent stress is healthy, keeping us on our toes. It's a form of stimulant. However, excessive stress damages both people and their decision-making powers. Too much stress arises from

- Time pressures and deadlines
- Multiple responsibilities
- Demands from other people
- Information bombardment
- Coping with change
- Meeting the expectations of superiors
- Our own perception of a situation – accurate or not

Countering the effects requires action such as

- Avoiding too many deadlines
- Making sure levels of responsibility are reasonable
- Not agreeing to other people's impossible demands
- Reducing the impact of information overload
- Anticipating, rather than just responding to, change

Checking whether we are seeing the world as it really is can be particularly valuable during decision making. Maybe we are seeing a situation far too negatively. Misconceptions can often create totally unnecessary self-imposed stress.

### IMPACT OF STRESS
Two other important effects of stress are

- Obstructing decisions
- Management by crisis

### Obstructing decisions
Stress commonly causes **decision paralysis**. This takes the form of delays or the avoidance of making a decision altogether.

We saw earlier how info freaks keep demanding ever more information. Often this is their response to stress and is why they hinder or prevent a decision from being made. They may well do so without even realizing it.

There may be such a serious penalty from whatever choice is made that it paralyses our ability to act. When that happens it reduces our own and other people's confidence in our judgement.

**Decisional conflict** occurs when we want simultaneously to accept and reject a particular course of action. A manager, for example, may want to sack someone yet personally like and respect them. This kind of clash of feelings creates indecision, promotes anxiety, and makes deciding more difficult.

The main way out of decisional conflict is to

●  make some definite choice that breaks the deadlock. No choice at all may only make matters worse.

### Management by crisis

By affecting the entire decision process, stress can prevent managers from responding carefully and systematically to making decisions. Instead, planning and any other ordered approaches are replaced by instinctive acts of desperation.

There is management by crisis when people keep saying there is not enough time to go through the basic decision stages properly. So there is little effort made to generate acceptable alternatives, only a cursory review of them. When the decision is finally made it may be forced by outside events rather than taken with due deliberation.

> **❝ The more you want people to have creative ideas and solve difficult problems, the less you can afford to manage them with terror. ❞**
>
> *Daniel Greenberg, Chairman, Electro Rent Corporation*

One of the most reliable findings from behavioural science is that when people are in a failure situation they suffer heightened tension and anxiety. The result is a natural tendency to revert to previously successful behaviour. This may be entirely the wrong response.

Organizations that provoke fear tend to exacerbate these tendencies. They are therefore more likely to experience management by crisis when people on the receiving end respond inappropriately to events.

A way of breaking into a management-by-crisis cycle is to

- Reduce the number or frequency of decisions – for example, by concentrating on one or two pressing ones
- Tightly control the decision process to ensure each stage is conducted with care
- Reduce a climate of fear being imposed by management style

## COPING WITH STRESS

> **❝ If I knew what I was so anxious about, I wouldn't be so anxious. ❞**
>
> *Mignon McLaughlin*

If we face an obstruction to decision making or management by crisis, it is rather late to do much to counter the effects. It is far better to watch the early warning signs and take action.

An important indicator of stress comes from physical symptoms. These may include sweating, dry mouth, palpitations, shallow breathing, tight feeling in the head, stomach cramps and so on. Each person reacts slightly differently. The bodily signs show us something is wrong.

Even if you cannot immediately alter the causes of stress you can do so indirectly by helping your body and mind.

So if you notice the signs of stress you might take a break, play a sport, have a long walk, do meditation or whatever.

If you cannot leave the work scene you can still find various ways to deal with stress, whether by having a break, going somewhere quiet for 10 minutes or meditating. Slow, deep breathing helps when you are unable to leave the room and must face a tough decision situation.

To cope with the psychological impact of stress on decision making

- DEVELOP a balanced picture
- SUSTAIN hope of finding a better alternative
- REALIZE there can be enough time for deliberation

### Balanced picture

People often dwell excessively on the risks of a decision without seeing the opportunities. We can avoid later problems by openly acknowledging the risks attached to our choices. Some of the techniques described in Chapter 5 are meant to help you produce a realistic picture of risk.

Certainly, ignoring the in-built uncertainty of all decision making is short-sighted and contributes to poor judgements. By confronting risks we can hope to understand and even overcome them. This is particularly true in organizations that are failing.

### A better alternative

If we believe a satisfactory alternative is possible, we will be more persistent in looking for it than if we have given up hope of finding one. When all the alternatives are presented in an entirely negative light there will be no great incentive for careful decision making.

A good way to escape this blind alley is to review objectives. The lack of any positive choices may suggest that a new approach is needed. By firming up aims and persevering we may well arrive at a far better selection of alternatives.

### Enough time

When we know we have adequate thinking time for a decision we are usually more confident and effective than if we feel rushed. A consistent, systematic series of decision steps is a great help in reconciling the time pressures.

The aim must be to make time somehow for the decision stages. In many organizations many of the so-called time pressures are self-imposed anxiety creators.

> **66 I've been working 15 or 16 hours a day trying to shorten working hours. 99**
>
> *Ioshio Yamuguchi, Japanese Labour Minister*

## BEHAVIOUR UNDER STRESS

The most popular ways people seem to cope with stress in their decision making are:

- BOLSTERING: Choosing the least objectionable alternative and rationalizing it as an acceptable choice
- CARRYING ON REGARDLESS: Complacently continuing whatever we have been doing despite the risks or possible pitfalls
- BLIND ACCEPTANCE: Uncritically adopting whatever new course of action is either most obvious or most strongly recommended
- PROCRASTINATION: Avoiding conflict by dithering, or shifting responsibility to someone else; also refusing to face the truth, however obvious it becomes
- OVERREACTION: Doing far more than necessary to deal with a problem; investing a disproportionate amount of energy, time or resources on a solution
- CAUTION: Searching carefully for any useful data and assimilating it before making a decision.

Of these patterns, the first five are defective. The sixth can also be the wrong approach, but generally only where a split-second decision is required. This is seldom the case in an organizational setting even if the decision is important.

## CHECKLIST

- Avoid making important decisions when under serious stress
- Respond to stress with relevant action
- Recognize decisional conflict and deal with it
- Break into a management-by-crisis cycle
- The amount of stress depends on what you think is at stake
- Watch for people's behaviour under stress
- Learn to recognize your own behaviour under stress
- Acknowledge risks; make informed choices to overcome them
- A positive view on finding alternatives aids the decision process

# 8

# CREATIVITY

A little boy once asked Walt Disney what he did. 'Do you draw Mickey Mouse?' The cartoon pioneer admitted he did not draw any more. 'Then do you think up all the jokes and ideas?' Disney had to confess he did not do that either. Finally the boy asked, 'Mr Disney, what exactly *do* you do?'

Disney explained: 'Sometimes I think of myself as a little bee. I go from one area of the studio to another and gather pollen and sort of stimulate everybody. I guess *that*'s the job I do.'

As Disney flitted round the studios he was contributing to better decision making by

- Challenging existing assumptions
- Questioning whether the most obvious solutions were the best
- Stimulating a fresh look at more creative alternatives
- Asking for more information
- Seeing the broader picture

### RESTRICTED ROLE
Management makes a virtue of monitoring, control and systematic planning. This is the atomistic approach, described in Chapter 6. It is preferred by some managers to a more holistic one in which more intangible factors play an important part.

**66 Nothing is more dangerous than an idea when it is the only one you have. 99**

*Emile Chartier, French philosopher*

Creativity is often restricted to the narrow role of generating a list of ideas. This is certainly important, though not its sole contribution.

Sadly, the demand for creativity in decision making often occurs only when an organization is facing serious failure. This is when the urge for newness suddenly goes to the top of the agenda. More of the same is unlikely to work and there is a demand to look afresh at the situation.

Why wait for a crisis? Rather than allow events to overtake us we need to

- Build creativity into all decision making and problem solving

Creativity can contribute to all eight stages of the decision process. Fresh ideas and new thinking are relevant to all of them, not merely to the obvious ones of creating alternatives or thinking up solutions.

### CREATIVE PEOPLE
When people are creative they

- Have lots of energy
- Willingly look beyond the obvious
- Stimulate each other to find new solutions
- Are persistent in pursuing their goals
- Take risks
- Act as if there is a better way

All of these may be important for reaching a sound decision. When people use them they begin tapping into their full potential. Decision making becomes a more rounded, realistic activity.

Since these behaviours are not easily either quantified or

controlled, creativity is too often relegated to a minor role. It is frequently dismissed as 'not business-like'.

Good management though, as Disney or any other effective leader demonstrates, means stimulating creativity, then reconciling it with organizational constraints that may seem to be pulling in an opposite direction.

## MORE TOOLS OF THE TRADE
We access our creativity in many ways. Some of the methods are now formalized and designed to stimulate.

- Fluency – producing a large number of ideas
- Flexibility – producing a wide variety of ideas
- Elaboration – developing or embellishing ideas
- Originality – finding ideas that are neither obvious nor overused
- Perspective – seeing the whole picture
- Sensitivity – contacting previously hidden thoughts
- Discrimination – selecting what will be most useful

To improve your decision making you may need to refine these skills or be able to encourage them in other people.

## FRESH ALTERNATIVES
Creativity has a special contribution at the point in the decision process where we must generate alternatives. These usually take the form of

- Different courses of action
- Likely causes
- Possible solutions
- Variety of outcomes

### Courses of action
Creativity is essential for forming a full picture of the possible courses of action we might take. As indicated

in Chapter 1, our natural tendency to use readily available information means we may easily neglect or ignore important alternatives.

Creativity can help force previously unacceptable courses of action to the surface to be fully considered for the first time. For example, when Ted Turner launched CNN, the international news service, many competitors had already rejected this course of action.

### Like causes

In problem solving we are often trying to unravel a cause and put a relevant solution in place. Even if the search is highly systematic, it may take a great deal of creativity to find it and then convince others of its validity.

For example, the Nobel scientist Richard Feynman was asked to help find the cause of the Saturn rocket tragedy in which several astronauts were killed. Despite a systematic search, it was Feynman who solved the puzzle creatively by identifying the failed 'O' rings, then demonstrated it convincingly on television using a glass of water and some ice cubes.

### Possible solutions

In solving problems we may sometimes need to come up with entirely fresh or creative answers. These may emerge from

- A systematic analysis
- Creative forms of working

In the latter, sudden leaps of insight may be how the correct solution is found.

When there are a variety of possible solutions we must decide which is best to implement. It may require considerable ingenuity and creative thinking to avoid rejecting workable solutions which initially pose major difficulties.

**Variety of outcomes**
All decision have uncertain outcomes and we may need a creative approach to identify them. Failure to consider possible outcomes may be extremely costly.

For example, the decision to build the Aswan dam has unexpectedly resulted in serious damage to much of Egypt's agriculture.

Since some outcomes are bizarre or extreme, it is only too easy to entirely disregard these. A creative approach ensures we at least consider them, even if we ultimately reject them.

## TECHNIQUES
Specific techniques for generating a more creative approach include

- Brainstorming

    enables groups to create a number of alternative ideas via uninhibited contributions. It works by encouraging group members to come up with as many ideas as possible. All ideas, however good or bad, are accepted and documented for evaluation later on. The ideas are then refined until one or two are identified as worth pursuing.

    It is most suited to open-ended or creative decisions

- Free association

    a way of letting the mind roam over a broad territory by linking one word, idea or concept with another in a chain; it can be a highly focused activity or a general way of exploring new possibilities.

- Mind mapping

  a visual way of tracking links between ideas in a creative, rather than linear way; suitable for many aspects of decision making from identifying new products to analysing problems; begins with a single word or concept written in the centre of the page from which others flow out like the branches of a tree; the pattern acquires a basic structure without conscious effort

- Collective notebook method

  each participant receives a notebook in which is included a description of some major issue; those participating record their thoughts and ideas about the problem over time, maybe a month; the books are collected and the ideas collated by a coordinator; the findings are then discussed in a creative session

- Checklists

  challenge us to think creatively in response to specific questions; designed to ensure we look at the problem or situation more systematically, such as

  > Could we do this another way?
  > Would it cost more if we did?
  > Are they more successful?
  > Why are they more successful?

  these lists work best when applied to straightforward situations; they are less successful when dealing with a number of intangible elements

- Role playing

  an unusual way of looking at a situation and gaining fresh insights; works well when trying to identify new alternatives, gain people's commitment to decisions and to trigger new thinking about an old problem

● Improvisation

forces people to stop being cerebral and to get in touch with solutions that are being ignored through excessive rationality; improvisations can be fun and surprisingly insightful

● Story telling

produces unexpected perspectives on a problem or decision through the medium of stories; these may be devised by an entire group, by two or three people or just one person; the shared experience can bring a new depth of thinking to a decision situation

● Drawing

a way of getting in touch with part of our brain that may not usually have a chance to contribute to a decision; using symbols or cartoons, for example, can throw new light on a decision and the choices

● Metaphors, analogies and images

by redefining the problem or decision in terms of a metaphor or analogy – for example, exploring a decision such as a takeover as 'like a marriage' – we may be helped to see the choices in more meaningful ways or ones that stimulate new thinking about the potential outcomes

All these techniques and many others attempt to use the brain's connective powers to see new possibilities.

Many of them are easy to use. Brainstorming, for example, is well entrenched in many companies. Others, like role playing or use of metaphors, may require some outside assistance to turn them into a real aid to the decision process.

> **66** The uncreative mind can spot wrong answers, but it takes a creative mind to spot wrong questions. **99**

## EACH OF US HAS IT

One of the myths of creativity is that only certain people have the ability to be inventive, imaginative and original. This is absolutely not so. We all possess the potential to be creative, and it is usually what brings us alive and makes us truly effective both as decision makers and human beings.

## CHECKLIST

- Creativity contributes to decision making by

    challenging assumptions and the most obvious solutions; stimulating more imaginative alternatives; asking for more information; seeing the broader picture

- Build creativity into all stages of decision making and problem solving

- When people are creative they

    have lots of energy; look beyond the obvious; stimulate new solutions; are persistent in pursuing their goals; take risks; act as if there is a better way

- Creative methods stimulate

    fluency; flexibility; elaboration; originality; perspective; sensitivity; discrimination

- creativity helps identify different courses of action, likely causes, possible solutions and outcomes

- techniques for creativity use the brain's connective powers to see new possibilities
- everyone can be creative in their decision making and in their life

---

**66 Being creative is like being in love!99**

*Woody Flowers, MIT*

# 9

# IMPLEMENTATION

> ❝ Nothing will ever be attempted if all possible objections must first be overcome. ❞
>
> **Dr Johnson**

The final stage of decision making is making it happen. This is much harder than choosing what to do which by comparison may be quick and fairly painless. To implement a decision you

- Anticipate problems
- Sell the decision and gain commitment
- Put a plan into effect.

When we make a decision we always need to know

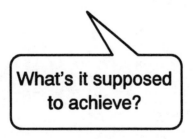

What's it supposed to achieve?

Too often managers rush into action without addressing this. They fear not taking an immediate decision will be construed as weakness or indecisiveness. In fact, a decision *not* to take action is sometimes just as important.

## ANTICIPATING PROBLEMS

Having made your decision you now have to carry it out. Unless circumstances have significantly altered or new information is available, changing your mind at this stage can be damaging.

**Decisional regret** is a common experience when people have made an important choice. They may immediately start seeking to alter it. The alternatives that were rejected may suddenly seem more attractive once viewed from an entirely different perspective.

---

**66 Once a decision was made I did not worry about it afterwards. 99**

*Harry S Truman*

---

Frequent changes of mind after a decision usually shows some part of the decision process has not been conducted thoroughly.

Decisional regret preys on our insecurity and can lead us to subvert perfectly workable plans. Once you have taken a decision look forward, not backwards. Once the decision is made, act as if it cannot be reversed.

Always assume:

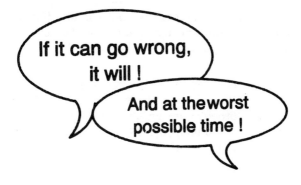

If it can go wrong, it will !

And at the worst possible time !

Taking this gloomy view and acting on it can help reduce the number of nasty surprises ahead. Identify difficult areas by continually asking 'what if?' questions and
be willing to think the unthinkable.

List as wide a range of problems as possible and evaluate
them. What are the chances of each occurring? Rank
them in terms of

- The **Likely**
- The **Serious**

You can then decide whether counter measures are
needed and, if so, which ones.

Anticipating potential problems is not a luxury. It is an
intrinsic part of implementation. It may well save your
plan from veering disastrously off course.

### Preventive and contingency action
**Preventive** action aims to keep the plan on course by
stopping the problem arising in the first place. One
example would be training operators of new equipment
before letting them use it.

**Contingency** action assumes something will go wrong. The consequences must be dealt with to protect the original plan by, for example, fitting a cut-off switch to equipment so it won't overheat even if the operator forgets to switch it off.

The more serious the potential problem, the more time should be spent reviewing

- What actions would stop this problem arising?
- What are the signs the problem has arisen or is about to do so?
- How can we eliminate the cause if the problem arises?
- If the problem cannot be eliminated what will minimize its impact?

## GENERATING COMMITMENT

An important part of implementation is gaining people's commitment to what has been decided:

- A decision may need sanctioning by a higher authority
- Other people such as employees may be affected and need to be persuaded to cooperate
- Resources may be required to finance the decision
- People's enthusiastic support for a decision may be needed

Gaining commitment can occur in many ways: through face-to face contact, in formal presentations, in written reports and so on.

You can encourage formal approval for a decision if you

- Show why the action deals with something important
- Only require a short-term commitment of re-

sources
- Allow variations in how the decision is implemented
- Show how the decision will achieve the outcome
- Clarify what improvement any change will bring
- Justify the costs
- Ensure that what is to be done can be easily understood
- Explain how the outcome can be evaluated

**Professionalize the material**

Many decisions first appear in a management report, initially as proposals. It is worth learning how to prepare a clear and compelling report. This should be readable and make a clear, logical case.

A careful eye on grammar, spelling and presentation is important. A grubby or illiterate proposal will certainly undermine your credibility. Unfair as it may seem, most of us are more easily influenced by the presentation of a point than by its content.

In putting your ideas across in a meeting, be as professional and succinct as you can. Be careful to present your ideas in words your audience will understand and to which they will respond. By becoming aware of their priorities you will be better placed to help them appreciate yours.

**Be enthusiastic**

To generate confidence in your decision or proposal, be positive and enthusiastic. Get to the point swiftly and avoid too much hesitation. Convince your audience you can both initiate the plan and carry it out.

**Concessions**

Not all aspects connected with the decision may be crucial. If you have to negotiate, use the less important parts with which to bargain. Decide in advance what concessions you are prepared to make.

### Prepare in depth

Know your information. If challenged you must show you understand all aspects of the decision and proposed action. It is particularly easy to lose track of detailed aspects if parts of the decision process have been delegated. Nevertheless, if the ultimate decision is yours, you must display a good knowledge of the detail.

### Timing

Be careful to present proposals when they might achieve the maximum effect. Avoid launching them when

- There are many issues already vying for attention
- A major issue is overshadowing everything
- Just before a holiday period or similar lay-offs

### Authority

Check you actually have authority to make the decision stick. If not, ask yourself who could stop you and why they would want to do so. Where the implementation extends beyond your authority you may need to 'sell' the idea to your superiors.

### Performance indicators

Establish a timetable and specific deadlines so you can monitor progress. Be willing to be flexible where it will support your general aim.

We have already seen the value of anticipating problems. Recognizing signs of potential danger will give you an effective early warning system.

### Being accountable

Clearly define people's roles within the implementation. Everyone involved should be aware of their responsibilities. This includes you.

### Give clear instructions

Many decisions go wrong simply because those on the receiving end do not grasp what is expected of them. It may be useful to have someone else read out any written instructions to check these cannot be misinterpreted.

Make clear what you want done, how, and by when. Modify your requirements if they prove unfeasible or impractical. Consultation is as important as clear instructions.

### Counter delays

To keep the action moving forward deal with delays promptly. Use contingency plans and be prepared to improvise. This may force you to re-evaluate some of your initial aims.

### Review

Once the plan is under way keep reviewing progress. Return to the original objectives and decide if they need modifying in the light of current progress.

Decision making and implementation is an evolving process. It is important, therefore, to be sensitive to new situations and challenges.

## CHECKLIST

- Inaction may sometimes be as important as action
- Implementation is a crucial part of decision making
- Do not let decisional regret upset your final choice
- Anticipate problems; assume that if it can go wrong, it will
- For each problem ask: How likely is it to occur? How serious would it be if it did?
- Take preventive action to keep the plan on course

- Use contingency action to minimize the impact of problems
- To gain commitment for the decision: present your case effectively; be enthusiastic; anticipate and pre-empt objections
- Check you have the authority to carry out a decision
- Monitor progress by establishing a timetable and clear deadlines
- Clarify who is responsible for what – including you
- Make sure your instructions are received and understood
- Be willing to modify requirements that prove impractical
- To keep the plan on course deal promptly with delays
- Review progress regularly, including the original objective

---

**66 When in doubt, jump!99**

*Malcolm Forbes*

---

# TEN DECISION LIFE-SAVERS

- Beware of over-reliance on instinct

  Gut feeling suggests we know the right choice to make. Instinct is usually best used, though, when you have plenty of facts and information. Some choices are 'counter intuitive'.

- Write it down

  Since many decisions involve juggling with lots of facts and feelings, making sense of them in your head can be difficult, if not impossible. Writing down the information in some systematic way, such as the pros and cons, may improve your handling of some choices.

- Stress warps judgement

  Strong feelings or potentially serious consequences can seriously distort decision making. Find ways to reduce stress through, for example, talking about the choice to someone else, allowing more time for deliberation or adopting relaxation methods such as breathing deeply several times to calm you at the point of decision.

- Clarify time scale

  Many choices do not require an immediate decision. You frequently have time to allow more information to accumulate before deciding. It is not being decisive to rush into a choice when more reflection or information might produce a better result.

- Simple statistics improve some choices

  We rarely know the full consequences of a decision. So most choices are based on our guess about the probabilities – the chance of something occurring. The human desire to make sense of things and see patterns where perhaps none exist can lead one astray. Simple statistical methods can aid many decisions.

- Use your brain

  It helps to sleep on a difficult decision before arriving at your final choice. Your brain is like a computer, able to sift complex facts and judgements without your conscious state interfering. You will often wake up the next day, clear about what to do.

- Employ available information

  Look for information that might contradict your point of view. Refusal to seek evidence that might show one is wrong is a common cause of poor decisions. If a choice has cost you a great deal of time and money it can be tempting to stick with it, even though the evidence suggests this is a wrong decision.

- The past is a poor predictor

  We cannot know the future which, by definition, has not yet happened. It is therefore tempting to rely on the past to tell us what the future holds. Because something has happened even many times before does not necessarily mean it will automatically occur again.

- Keep money in perspective

Reducing all choices to a question of money is misguided, even if you are an accountant or treasury official. Many choices involve consequences that are not readily or appropriately reduced to money terms.

- Make it your choice

  A group may become so committed to a choice that it unconsciously combines to reject anything that contradicts what it wants to do. Similarly, an authority figure can sometimes influence decisions inappropriately, when more objective reasoning would suggest a different choice. Make sure when you make a choice that it is yours and not someone else's.

## PERFECT COMMUNICATIONS

Andrew Leigh and Michael Maynard

Taking for their main topics impact, spoken communication, group communication, honesty, feedback, building relationships, telephone and written communication, creativity and conflict resolution, the authors pilot the reader swiftly and surely through the do's and don'ts and provide all the information necessary to ensure that communications will be perfect whatever the subject and whoever one is communicating with.

£5.99 (p)     0 7126 5602 2

## THE PERFECT PRESENTATION

Andrew Leigh and Michael Maynard

Many people are terrified of making a presentation in public, while others are just unsure of how to go about it effectively. But the ability to do it successfully can make all the difference to your personal career, and to the business prospects of your firm. This book provides a sure-fire method based on the 5 P's of Perfect Presentation: Preparation, Purpose, Presence, Passion and Personality. It is an excellent, hands-on guide which takes the reader step by step to success in one of the most important business skills.

£5.99 (p)     0 7126 5536 0

# THE OC

## *The Outsider*

Based on the television series created by
Josh Schwartz including the episode 'Pilot',
written by Josh Schwartz

# LEVEL 2

**Adapted by:** Patricia Reilly

**Fact Files written by:** Jacquie Bloese

**Commissioning Editor:** Jacquie Bloese

**Designer:** Dawn Wilson

**Picture research:** Emma Bree

**Photo credits:**

Cover and inside images courtesy of Warner Bros.

**Page 10:** Design Pix/Punchstock.

**Page 52:** Stockbyte; T. Hemmings/Corbis.

**Page 53:** N. Ney, J. Springer Collection/Corbis; F. Brown/Getty Images.

Published by Scholastic Ltd.

Mary Glasgow Magazines (Scholastic Ltd.)
Euston House
24 Eversholt Street
London NW1 1DB

Printed in Singapore

# *Contents*

THE C

## SANDY COHEN
Sandy is an attorney.

## JIMMY AND JULIE COOPER
Marissa's mom and dad.

## SUMMER ROBERTS
Lives: Newport Beach
Problems? Which dress to wear …!
Dreams of … cute guys, parties and shopping!
Boyfriend? No-one special.

## MARISSA COOPER
Lives: Newport Beach, next door to the Cohens'
Problems? She's bored and wants to escape. She's worried about her father, doesn't like her mother and drinks too much sometimes.
Dreams of … a new life.
Boyfriend? Luke – for six years.

## RYAN ATWOOD
Lives: Chino
Problems? Lots! His dad's in prison, and his mom, Dawn, drinks too much. His brother Trey is always in trouble too.
Dreams of … leaving Chino and having a real family.
Girlfriend? Theresa is his ex-girlfriend.

4

# UTSIDER

## LUKE WARD

Luke has been Marissa's boyfriend for six years. He's rich and popular.

## KIRSTEN COHEN

## SETH COHEN

Lives: Newport Beach, next door to Marissa
Problems? He hates Newport and he doesn't have any real friends.
Dreams of … sailing to Tahiti with Summer Roberts. (But she doesn't know yet!)
Girlfriend? Not yet …

## PLACES

Chino A poor town, an hour away from Newport Beach. Ryan's family live here.

Newport Beach A rich town by the sea. There are lots of rich kids, big houses and expensive cars.

# Chapter 1
## 'You're under arrest!'

'My life is hell!' Ryan thought. Most days weren't good, but today was worse than usual. He walked out of the corner shop with a packet of cigarettes. Sixteen-year-old Ryan Atwood lived in Chino, California. Eighty kilometres away, in Orange County, there were beautiful Pacific beaches and very rich people. Chino was a different world. The Chino streets were poor and dirty. No one had any money and at night there was always trouble. Police cars were never far away. It was all Ryan knew – and he hated it.

'Hi!' His oldest friend, Theresa, was sitting outside her house. She smiled at Ryan. For a while in high school, Theresa was Ryan's girlfriend. But, for now, they were just friends – good friends.

'I got some cigarettes,' Ryan said. He gave her a

cigarette and sat down.

'Are you OK?' Theresa knew things were always hard for Ryan at home.

'Trey didn't come home until this morning and he was really drunk. Then A.J. hit me ...,' Ryan said and then he stopped. Two houses further down the street he could hear his mom, Dawn, and her new boyfriend, A.J. They were fighting again. Now that his dad was in prison, his mom usually had a boyfriend. Ryan thought A.J. was the worst. A.J. didn't have a job and Dawn paid for everything. She often drank all day and didn't go to work. A.J. didn't want Trey and Ryan around. Now Trey, Ryan's older brother, often stayed out all night.

'It's A.J.'s fault that Trey doesn't come home. Now I've got nobody,' Ryan thought. 'I want to get out of Chino.' Ryan dreamed of a better life. He knew that he could never have it in Chino.

'Tonight, let's try and forget all of that,' Theresa said.

'Do you want to stay here? You can sleep on the sofa.'

A.J. and his mom were still fighting. Ryan didn't want to go home. He smiled at Theresa and followed her inside.

\*\*\*

'Ryan, wake up!' Ryan sat up suddenly and looked around. There was nobody there.

'Was I dreaming?' he asked himself.

'Get up.' It was Trey. He was standing outside at the window. Ryan looked at his watch. Two o'clock in the *morning*? Why was his brother there?

'Come with me.'

'It's two in the morning. Where?' asked Ryan.

'I can't go home and I can't stay here. Come on,' Trey said.

'Ok ... I'll be out in a minute.'

Ryan got dressed. 'I won't leave a note for Theresa,' he thought. 'I'll be back in a few hours. I can explain later.'

He met Trey outside. 'Where are we going?' he asked.

'I can go out with my little brother for some fun, can't I? We're going to a party,' Trey said.

Ryan decided to go with Trey. They walked through the back streets until they came to a strange house.

'This isn't where Trey usually hangs out,' Ryan thought. He went in after Trey.

'Atwood. You came.' A guy came over to Trey. Trey went with him into another room.

Ryan wasn't surprised. Trey often left him alone. He went into the kitchen and got a beer from the fridge. He started to drink it but then a big guy took it from him angrily.

'That's one dollar. The drinks aren't free. Not for Trey Atwood's friends,' he said.

'What does he mean?' Ryan thought. The guy didn't seem to like his brother. Ryan paid and left the kitchen fast. He wanted to be alone. He went into the bathroom, closed the door and drank his beer.

'Why is my life always difficult?' he thought. 'I've always dreamed of leaving Chino and having a real family. But it never happens.'

Suddenly he heard loud, angry voices in the room next to the bathroom.

'Five thousand. By tomorrow morning,' someone shouted.

'Five thousand? Five thousand what? *Dollars*?' Ryan didn't understand.

'I mean it, Atwood. No money, you're dead!'

'You'll get your money,' Trey shouted.

Trey was in trouble. Ryan was frightened. He didn't know what to do.

'I could climb out of the window … but I can't just leave Trey. He's my family.' Ryan left the bathroom and went back to the kitchen. Trey walked in.

'Let's go,' he said.

They left. Ryan didn't know what to do. Trey didn't know that he knew about the money. Ryan looked at his brother. Trey looked worried. Ryan knew that the people from the party were dangerous.

'Trey can't get five thousand dollars by tomorrow. And mom doesn't have it. They'll kill him,' he thought. The idea was terrible.

'I'm sorry,' Trey said.

'For what?' Ryan asked. But he already knew the answer.

'You know. Everything,' Trey said. Ryan knew Trey wanted to be the perfect big brother, but he was always in trouble.

'Do you think we'll ever get out of here?' Ryan asked.

'Now? No.'

'Yeah, it's a dream,' Ryan said.

'Listen to me,' said Trey. 'I haven't learned much in my life, but I know one thing. Dreams don't come true.'

'He's right,' Ryan thought. 'Not in Chino.'

'We're not going home,' Trey said suddenly.

'What are we going to do?' Ryan asked.

'Have you ever stolen a car?'

'Stolen … a car? No,' he said.

'There,' Trey said and pointed to a car. 'That's ours. We're getting out of here.'

Ryan couldn't believe it. Was Trey joking? But then he remembered the money and the guy from the party. He understood. Trey was leaving Chino and he was taking Ryan with him. Could he leave Chino? He was frightened. He looked at his brother.

'Are you sure?' he asked.

'Come on!' Trey said. Quickly he broke the car window. The two brothers jumped in.

'I wanted to get out of Chino,' Ryan thought, 'but not in a stolen car. This isn't going to end well.'

They started to drive down the road. Trey laughed. Ryan couldn't believe it.

'We're free,' he thought. 'We've done it. We're leaving.'

Suddenly he heard a police car. He looked out the back window and saw the red and blue lights. Trey drove faster.

'Don't worry, we'll escape,' he shouted. He almost crashed into two cars which were passing in front of them. Ryan held onto the seat. Then Trey nearly hit another car. The police car wasn't following them now.

'We did it!' Trey shouted.

But the next minute there were more police cars. Two, three, four? Ryan wasn't sure. Trey tried to lose them, but a police car crashed into their car.

'Oh, no!' Ryan thought. 'My life will never be the same again.'

The police got out of their car and ran over. Trey got out, with his arms above his head. This wasn't his first arrest. Ryan was frightened. He didn't move. Someone handcuffed Trey and put him into the back of a police car.

'Will they arrest me too? Will I go to prison? Or Juvie*?' Ryan thought, worried.

'Get out!' one of the police shouted. 'You're under arrest!'

He handcuffed Ryan. It hurt. Then Ryan got into another police car. He thought about Theresa. 'She'll wake up and I won't be there. She won't know what's happened. I didn't even leave a note.'

As they were driving away, Ryan could see Trey's face in the other police car.

'Will I ever see Trey again?' he asked himself, sadly. He felt more alone than ever.

* 'Juvie' is a kind of prison centre for young people under the age of 18.

# CHAPTER 2
## A Pucci dress

Marissa Cooper was sixteen, beautiful and popular. She lived in one of the biggest and most expensive houses in Newport, Orange County. Marissa's life seemed perfect, but she wasn't happy.

'Newport's always the same. Nothing ever changes,' thought Marissa. She was with her best friend, Summer.

'Every year is the same. I go to school with the same people,' Marissa thought. 'We do the same things. I've had the same best friend since I was five. And the same boyfriend since I was ten.'

Her boyfriend, Luke, was tall and good-looking. Today he was at the beach with the other guys. But Marissa didn't want to think about Luke. She wasn't listening to Summer. She didn't feel very well.

'I drank too much last night,' she thought, 'but I don't care. I feel happy when I drink. I don't feel bored. I don't feel worried about everything. I can just have fun.'

'Coop*,' said Summer, 'What are you wearing to the fashion show on Saturday?'

'I don't know,' said Marissa. There was a fashion show in Newport every year to make money for poor children. This year, Marissa and Summer were both appearing in the show.

'What are you wearing to Holly's beach party?' asked Summer.

Marissa didn't want to go to Holly's party. She was tired of all these summer beach parties. Sometimes she just wanted to stay at home, but she couldn't say no to her friends. She never said no.

---

* Marissa's surname is Cooper. Summer calls her 'Coop'.

'Marissa? Hello? Let's go shopping,' said Summer.

\*\*\*

'This dress is perfect for you,' said Summer. She was holding a black dress.

'Yes,' thought Marissa, 'Perfect and boring. I don't want to be perfect. I want to be myself.' She picked up a beautiful Pucci dress which had lots of different colours in it.

'What do you think?' she asked Summer.

'It's cute, but …'

'But what?' Marissa felt angry. She knew that Summer thought the dress was wrong for her. 'I like punk music and I want to be me,' she thought. 'I want to be free.'

Summer knew something was wrong. 'It's cute. You should totally buy it,' she said. 'Let's go and pay.'

\*\*\*

'I'm sorry, miss, your credit card isn't working.' The shop assistant handed back Marissa's card. Marissa was surprised. Her dad *always* paid her credit card bill. She could usually buy anything she wanted.

'Don't worry, I'll pay,' said Summer.

'No, that's OK … I'll come back later,' said Marissa. She was worried. The card didn't work. Why? Then she remembered something.

'Those men who came to the house yesterday … . They looked like police,' she thought. 'Why did they want to see Dad? Maybe something is wrong.'

\*\*\*

'Hi! Did you have a good time?' Marissa's dad, Jimmy, asked when Marissa came home.

'Yeah. Summer and I went shopping,' Marissa said. She waited for him to ask, *'What did you buy?'* He always asked. But this time he didn't say anything.

'The credit card didn't work,' Marissa said. 'Can I have some money?'

'No!' Jimmy shouted. 'I'm not a bank!'

Marissa wanted to cry. 'Dad never shouts at me,' she thought. 'I'm sure he's in trouble, but he won't talk about it. He usually tells me everything.'

Just then the phone rang. Her younger sister, Kaitlin, called to her. 'It's Luke!'

Marissa left her dad's office and went to the phone.

'Do you want to hang out tonight?' Luke asked.

'OK,' Marissa said. 'Another boring night in boring Newport,' she thought.

\*\*\*

'Marissa, come and try on some dresses for the fashion show.' It was her mom, Julie.

'Here, try this,' Julie said. Marissa put on the dress. It was the same as the black dress in the shop.

'Yes, that looks fantastic,' her mom was saying. 'OK,

next.' Julie pointed to a pink dress.

'I like the black one,' Marissa said.

'Marissa,' said her mom, 'you must have choices. Now try this on.' Marissa tried the dress.

It looked OK.

'Oh, no …,' said Julie. 'It's too small.'

'Too small?' thought Marissa, 'Maybe I should lose a few kilos.' Marissa was thin, perhaps too thin. She tried another dress.

'No,' said Julie, 'It's too …'

Just then, Jimmy came in. He smiled at Marissa.

'You look beautiful,' he said.

'Jimmy, she has to look perfect,' Julie said. 'And that dress …'

But Marissa didn't want to try any more dresses. 'I think the black dress is fine, mom,' she said.

'You're impossible!' Julie shouted and she left angrily.

'She just wants the best for you,' Jimmy said. 'I'm sorry I shouted. You know I love you. Buy that dress.' He gave her some money.

'Thanks, dad. I love you too.' Marissa knew that something was still wrong, but, for a moment, she felt happy again.

Marissa looked at her watch. Luke was coming in two hours, but she didn't want to see him. She reached for the phone.

'Luke? I can't hang out tonight. I've got to stay at home with Kaitlin,' she said.

'I've never lied to Luke before,' Marissa thought. 'I never change our plans.'

'Do you want me to come over?' Luke asked.

'No, you hang out with the others. Have fun. I'll call you later,' Marissa said.

She went back to the shop and bought the Pucci dress. When she got home, her dad was waiting.

'What did you buy?' he asked.

Marissa ran to her bedroom and put on the dress.

'You look great,' Jimmy said.

Marissa knew he was surprised by the dress. But she didn't care. She felt happy. Her dad was being her dad again.

*** 

Marissa was alone in her bedroom.

'I'm never alone,' she thought. 'Usually I'm with Luke or Summer or the girls.'

She put on a *Clash* CD and danced to her favourite song. She felt really free. She looked at herself in the mirror. Her dress was beautiful and for once, she felt like herself.

'Maybe things *can* change,' she thought.

Just then, her mobile phone rang. It was Luke. Marissa didn't answer. Tonight she was waiting for something new.

# CHAPTER 3
## Not in Chino anymore ...

'Atwood. Visitor.'

Ryan was in Juvie. 'Who's come to visit me?' he thought as he followed his guard through the prison. 'Nobody knows I'm here.'

They went into a small room. A man was sitting at a table and reading some papers. He was about forty and he was wearing an expensive suit. Ryan guessed the papers were about him.

The man looked up. 'Hi, Ryan. I'm Sandy Cohen. I'm your attorney.'

'Where's my brother?' Ryan asked.

'Trey? Trey's over eighteen. Trey stole a car. Trey's in prison,' Sandy said.

Ryan didn't say anything.

'I can remember what it's like. Dad away, mom never around,' Sandy thought. 'At one time that was my life too.'

He looked at the papers. 'Ryan, you're a clever kid,' he said.

It was true. Ryan didn't always go to school, but his test results were over 90%.

'Have you thought about your future?' Sandy asked.

'I read about the future,' Ryan said. 'Soon people will live to be a hundred, but they'll have to work until they're eighty.'

Sandy smiled. Ryan was clever, maybe too clever.

'Look, I can help you. You can get out of Juvie. You'll get probation,' Sandy said. 'But you should have a plan, a dream …'

'In Chino, you don't have dreams,' said Ryan. 'Dreams don't come true.'

* * *

Sandy and Ryan were waiting for Dawn outside Juvie. Finally she arrived in her old car. She was driving too fast and she seemed a bit drunk.

'Hi, Mrs Atwood. I'm Ryan's attorney,' Sandy said.

But Dawn didn't answer. 'Get in the car, Ryan,' she said.

'Ryan, here's my card,' Sandy said. 'There's my phone number. If you need anything, call me.'

Ryan was surprised. 'Nobody's offered to help me before,' he thought.

Sandy watched Ryan and Dawn drive away. He knew Dawn was drunk.

'I hope Ryan will be OK,' he thought.

* * *

At home, Dawn was shouting. 'I can't do this anymore, Ryan.' She got another drink.

'I'm sorry,' Ryan said.

'I don't want you in this house. I want you to leave!' Dawn shouted.

'You heard your mom. Get your things and go,' A.J. said.

'This isn't your house,' Ryan said.

And then they started fighting. A.J. hit Ryan hard and Ryan fell to the floor. His mother didn't say anything and she didn't look at him. Slowly he got up and went to his room. He put some clothes in a bag and left. He got on his bike and went to the pay phone outside the supermarket. He called everyone he knew, but no one was home. Then he found Sandy's card.

'I don't have a choice,' he thought. He picked up the phone.

*\*\**

As Sandy and Ryan drove through Newport, Ryan couldn't believe his eyes.

'The houses … the cars,' he thought. 'These people are rich. Really rich.'

Sandy parked outside one of the biggest houses.

'Could you wait in the car?' Sandy said. 'I've got to talk to my wife, Kirsten.'

Inside, Sandy was explaining.

'He stole a car and you brought him *home*?' Kirsten said angrily.

'It's only for the weekend. Child Services* opens on Monday,' Sandy said.

'OK, but he sleeps in the pool house,' said Kirsten finally.

Their son, Seth, walked in. 'Who's sleeping in the pool house?' he asked.

'Ask your father!' said Kirsten.

'Seth, there's this kid, Ryan. I'm his attorney. He's staying for the weekend. He doesn't come from a good family and he doesn't have anywhere to stay,' Sandy explained.

Seth thought about this for a moment.

'Interesting … like a little brother,' he said.

'Not exactly. He's your age,' Sandy said.

'A sixteen-year-old guy? Thanks, dad. That's great. I'm sure we'll be best friends,' Seth said. Seth wasn't happy. He didn't really like most guys his age.

'Seth, wait,' Sandy said. But Seth went to his bedroom to read his new comics.

Outside, Ryan was bored. He decided to have a cigarette. He walked down to the road. Next door, Marissa came out of her house. Suddenly, she saw Ryan. Their eyes met and she smiled.

'She's so beautiful,' thought Ryan.

'Who are you?' asked Marissa.

Ryan tried to be cool. 'Anyone you want,' he said.

'That wasn't very cool. But he's so … different,' thought Marissa. 'Can I have a cigarette?' she asked.

Ryan gave her a cigarette. His hand touched hers – just for a moment.

'Wow, this is better than any new dress,' thought Marissa. 'So, what are you doing here?' she asked.

* Child Services is a place which helps children and young people with problems.

'I stole a car and crashed it. Well, my brother stole it. He's in prison and I'm on probation. My mom didn't want me at home anymore so Mr Cohen invited me to stay,' he said.

Marissa laughed. Ryan was surprised.

'No, really. You're the Cohens' cousin from Boston, aren't you?' she said.

Ryan understood. She wasn't laughing at him. She just didn't believe him.

'Yeah … Boston,' he said. He wanted to ask her name, but just then Sandy came out of the house.

'Hi, Mr Cohen. I've just met your nephew,' Marissa said.

Sandy looked at Ryan quickly, and then understood. 'Ah, yes, my favourite nephew, Ryan. From Seattle,' he said.

'Seattle?' said Marissa, surprised.

'My dad lives there,' said Ryan quickly. 'Mom lives in Boston.'

Sandy decided to change the conversation.

'We're all really excited about the fashion show tomorrow,' he said.

Marissa turned to Ryan. 'Why don't you come along?' she said. She smiled.

'Wow,' thought Ryan, 'She's … fantastic. I've never met anyone like her before.'

Just then Luke arrived in his car.

'Bye,' said Marissa, as she got in.

'Who was that?' Luke asked.

'Nobody. Just the Cohens' cousin,' said Marissa. But inside she was thinking: *He was something else. He was different.*

\*\*\*

Sandy and Ryan went into the house. Ryan looked around. He couldn't believe it. The house was … beautiful. Sandy took him through the kitchen and outside to the pool house. There he met Kirsten.

'Welcome to our home,' she said. She tried to smile.

'She doesn't want me here,' Ryan thought.

Sandy and Kirsten said good night and left Ryan alone. He undressed and got into bed. The room was quiet.

As he fell asleep, Ryan thought about his mom, dad and Trey. 'Will I ever see them again?' he asked himself. He didn't know the answer.

# CHAPTER 4
## The outsiders

Seth couldn't sleep.

'Who is this strange kid?' he thought. 'Maybe he's dangerous. He's been to Juvie.' Seth didn't like the kids in Newport. They thought he was a geek. He was too different. Seth hated Newport.

Downstairs, he could hear his parents talking about Ryan.

'He can only stay for the weekend,' Kirsten was saying. She stopped suddenly. 'But did you see his eyes, Sandy? He looked so …'

'Sad?' Sandy said.

'I know how it feels to be sad and alone,' Seth thought. 'Maybe Ryan and I can be friends. We can do things together. Hang out. Look for girls … That will be cool.'

'Where's his family?' Kirsten asked.

'His brother's in prison,' said Sandy. 'And his mom … she drinks. She didn't want him at home anymore. Ryan's not dangerous. He's just a kid with nowhere to go.'

Seth couldn't believe it. Ryan's life sounded so different to his.

'What will I say to Ryan?' he asked himself. 'I need a plan. I need to be cool.'

Seth thought about his plan to sail to Tahiti with Summer Roberts. Seth was in love with Summer, but she had no idea. He called his boat *Summer Breeze* after her. But Ryan wasn't Summer. Seth had no plan for Ryan.

'I could show him my comics. But maybe he doesn't think comics are cool,' Seth thought. 'Or we could listen to music.' Seth had lots of music. He loved punk and indie rock.

'What do other guys listen to?' he thought. More than ever, Seth felt like an outsider. He wanted to run away, but he couldn't. He had nowhere to go.

'Maybe we could be friends. Maybe it'll work,' he thought just before he fell asleep.

\*\*\*

Seth slowly got dressed. He still didn't have a plan. Downstairs, there was a message from his mom in the kitchen.

'Great,' he thought. 'Mom's in the office. Dad's gone shopping. *I* have to show Ryan round the house and make breakfast.' Seth wasn't very happy. 'Why have mom and dad left me alone with Ryan?' he thought.

\*\*\*

Outside in the pool house, Ryan woke up. At first, he didn't know where he was. And then he remembered everything. He got dressed and walked across to the house. There was a guy about his age in the living room. He was playing a PlayStation game.

'Hi,' the guy said. He didn't stop playing.

'Hi,' said Ryan. So this was the Cohens' son … .

'Do you want to play?' Seth asked.

'OK,' said Ryan.

When Sandy came home, Ryan and Seth were still on the PlayStation. He couldn't believe it. They were having fun together!

'Do you want to play *Auto Theft?*' Seth asked 'It's really cool. You steal cars …' Suddenly Seth remembered. *Ryan stole a car*. Ryan looked angry.

'I didn't mean …' Seth didn't know what to say. 'That's it. Ryan will hate me now,' he thought.

Sandy came into the room. 'So you two have met,' said Sandy. 'It's a beautiful day. Seth, why don't you show Ryan around Newport?'

\*\*\*

Seth and Ryan were sailing past Newport Beach on *Summer Breeze*. Ryan was thinking about home. Seth was trying to think of something to say.

'Ryan probably thinks I'm a geek. I have to say something,' he thought. 'So, do you like sailing?' he asked.

'Yeah,' said Ryan.

'This isn't working,' thought Seth. 'Could I tell him about Summer? About my plan to sail to Tahiti?'

Ryan was still thinking about Chino. He wasn't listening to Seth. He felt bad. He knew Seth was really trying. Seth looked at Ryan. 'I've got this plan,' he said. 'Maybe you'll think it's stupid, but … Next July, I want to sail to Tahiti. I can do it in forty-four days, maybe forty-two.'

Ryan didn't know what to say. 'I've never met anyone with real plans before,' he thought. 'Wow, that sounds great,' he said.

Ryan couldn't believe it. Seth had dreams. And he believed in them. He wanted to know more.

'That's a long time to be alone,' Ryan said.

'I'll have Summer with me,' Seth said without thinking.

Ryan looked at the name of the boat. 'You're going to Tahiti on this boat?' he said, surprised.

'No. Summer. She's a girl that I like. That's why the boat's name is *Summer Breeze*.'

'Wow,' said Ryan, 'She must be happy about that.'

'She has no idea,' said Seth. 'We go to the same school, but I've never spoken to her.'

Now Ryan felt bad. They didn't speak as they sailed back to the beach.

\*\*\*

Sandy came down to the beach to meet them.

'So, Seth … we're all going to the fashion show around seven,' he said.

'Have fun,' Seth said.

Ryan was surprised. 'He doesn't want to go. Why?' he asked himself.

'Well, Ryan has to go. Marissa invited him,' Sandy said.

'Marissa invited him?' Seth said, surprised. 'I've lived next door to Marissa all my life. She's never invited me to anything. Not even a birthday party.'

Now Ryan understood. 'Seth feels like an outsider here. Just like me,' he thought. He wanted to help.

'Seth … maybe Summer will be there,' he said.

'Summer? Summer is Marissa's best friend … . Interesting … . Seven o'clock, you said?' Seth started walking up the hill.

'Summer? Who's Summer?' asked Sandy.

'Don't worry about it,' said Ryan.

\*\*\*

Marissa watched Seth, Sandy and Ryan from her
bedroom window. She couldn't stop thinking about Ryan.
There was something different about him.

'I'll see him later,' she thought.

# CHAPTER 5
## The fashion show

Marissa was putting on her Pucci dress when her mobile phone rang. It was Summer.

'Coop, I need help!' she said.

'What's happened?' asked Marissa.

'My dress … I can't wear it … It's totally the wrong colour for me. Coop, what do I do?' said Summer.

'Don't worry,' said Marissa. 'I bought that Pucci dress the other day. It'll look good on you. I'll bring it.'

'Coop, you're the best,' said Summer. 'See you later.'

Marissa looked down at the dress. She didn't need it now. She had a new escape. Ryan.

\*\*\*

Next door, Ryan was wearing one of Sandy's suits and thinking about Marissa. He remembered her smile. He felt lost in Newport, but there was something different about her … .

Sandy put his head round the door. 'So, did you and Seth have a good time today?'

Ryan didn't know what to say. Seth was a bit strange, but he liked him.

'He's cool,' he said.

'Really?' said Sandy. He was happy.

Ryan looked at himself in the mirror. He looked great. 'Maybe I'll be OK here,' he thought.

\*\*\*

'Welcome to the dark side,' Seth said to Ryan. They were outside the Regis Hotel. Rich, beautiful people were everywhere.

'Wow,' Ryan thought, as they walked in, 'I've never seen a place like *this*.' The hotel was big and expensive. It had a big outside pool and a bar. You could see the beach. Ryan turned to Seth, but Seth wasn't there.

A beautiful older woman walked up to him. 'So, you're the cousin from Boston,' she said, smiling. 'Do you like Newport? How long are you staying?'

The woman talked non-stop. Ryan tried to go to the bar, but everyone wanted to talk to him. They all asked questions. *Are you from Canada? Boston? Seattle?*

Another woman stopped him. 'Ryan, there's someone I want you to meet.'

She took his arm. 'Marissa, this is Ryan,' she said.

Marissa turned round and looked at Ryan. He looked even better than yesterday.

'Hi, Ryan. Nice to meet you,' she said. She didn't want to seem too interested.

Ryan understood. 'Nice to meet you, too,' he said. He looked around the room, at all the people.

'So, what do you think of Newport?' Marissa asked.

Ryan wanted to tell her. He felt lost but it was great to see her again. But then Marissa's dad came up and Ryan didn't have time to answer.

\*\*\*

Ryan and Seth were by the bar when Luke came to get a drink.

'Maybe I can make some new friends,' thought Seth. 'I know the other guys don't usually talk to me. And the guys like Luke … they're the worst. But maybe things have changed.' He decided to try.

'Hi, Luke,' he said quietly.

'Get lost, geek,' said Luke and walked off.

'My holidays were great, too,' said Seth. 'Some things are never going to change,' he thought.

Ryan felt sorry for Seth. He understood why Seth didn't want to go to Newport parties.

'Look!' Seth suddenly said. 'No, don't look!'

'Seth, what are you talking about?' asked Ryan.

'Summer. Over there with Marissa.'

Ryan looked. Summer was just as beautiful as Marissa.

Summer was looking at Ryan from the other side of the pool.

'Who's that?' she asked Marissa. 'He's cute!'

'I don't really know,' said Marissa.

'Well, I plan to find out!' Summer smiled.

\*\*\*

The fashion show was about to start. Marissa stood in front of everyone on the catwalk.

'Thank you all for coming,' she said. 'Every year we have this fashion show to make money for poor kids. We couldn't do it without your help. Now enjoy the show!'

Summer was the first girl to come down the catwalk. She looked great in Marissa's Pucci dress.

'Look at that dress,' said Seth. 'It's perfect for Tahiti!'

But Ryan could only think about Marissa.

\*\*\*

Marissa and Summer were in the girls' bathroom. 'Look what I stole …,' Summer laughed. She had two glasses of champagne.

'Look what I stole.' Marissa opened her bag. Inside there was a bottle of vodka. The girls laughed and drank the champagne.

'This is fun,' thought Marissa. 'The show is going well *and* Ryan's here.'

\*\*\*

Next it was Marissa's turn on the catwalk.

'She's so beautiful,' Ryan thought. He couldn't stop looking at her. Their eyes met. But then Luke and his friends started laughing and shouting.

'Where do they think they are? A football game?!' thought Ryan.

Luke was watching Ryan. He saw that Ryan was looking at Marissa. He didn't like it at all … .

\*\*\*

Ryan was in the bathroom. He was drying his hands when a man ran in. Ryan saw that it was Jimmy Cooper, Marissa's dad. His eyes were red and he seemed very upset.

'Maybe life isn't so perfect here,' Ryan thought.

\*\*\*

The show was over and everyone was leaving. Ryan followed Seth outside. Summer ran up to Ryan and touched his arm.

'Where are you going?' she asked.

Ryan didn't know what to say.

'My friend Holly is having a party in her parents' beach house … if you want to come. I'm Summer,' she smiled and walked away.

Ryan couldn't believe it. A beach house? He wasn't in Chino anymore … .

'Marissa will probably be there,' he thought. 'Let's go to that party,' he said to Seth.

'No,' said Seth.

'But Summer invited me,' Ryan said.

'Summer invited … you?' said Seth. The girl that he loved was interested in Ryan.

Ryan understood. 'No … *us*. She asked for you,' he said.

'She did? Are you sure?' said Seth, surprised. Summer and her friends were getting into a car. They called to the boys and Seth went over. Ryan followed. As they were getting in, Ryan saw Marissa. She was coming out of the hotel with Luke.

'Why are you looking at that guy?' Luke asked.

'I'm not. I'm with you,' said Marissa and she kissed him. But she watched as Ryan disappeared into the night.

# CHAPTER 6
## 'Welcome to the O.C.'

'Come on, Marissa,' Luke said. They were kissing in the back of his car, but Luke wanted more.

'Luke, no,' Marissa laughed.

'Six years. Will you ever …?' he asked.

'Not here. Not now,' said Marissa. She didn't want to talk about it now.

'You always say that!' said Luke angrily.

'Come on. Let's go to Holly's party. Everyone will be there,' Marissa said.

Luke drove to the party. They didn't speak.

\*\*\*

'Welcome to the dark side,' Ryan said to Seth as they walked into Holly's beach house.

'What a party!' Ryan thought. The music was loud. There were kids everywhere, drinking, dancing, smoking … .

'Do you want a beer?' someone shouted.

'OK,' said Ryan.

'Err … yes, I mean … yeah,' said Seth. They took their drinks. It was Seth's first drink ever.

\*\*\*

Marissa was with the girls. She was drinking vodka.

'Look who I invited,' said Summer and pointed to Ryan.

'He's cute,' Holly smiled.

Marissa turned to see who they were talking about. It was Ryan. 'He is cute. He's different. And nobody knows anything about him,' she thought. She turned back. She didn't want Ryan to know she was looking.

'I'm going to have some fun with him,' laughed Summer.

Marissa had another drink.

\*\*\*

Luke was talking to Nikki - a cute girl who seemed to like him.

'It's beautiful, isn't it? The sea, the beach …,' she said.

Where was Marissa? Luke looked around. He couldn't see her.

'Do you want to go down to the beach?' he asked Nikki.

'But what about your girlfriend?'

'Don't worry,' said Luke. Nikki took his arm and they went outside.

Ryan watched them. 'Why is Luke leaving Marissa? Why is he going outside with another girl?' he thought.

Across the room, the girls were drinking and laughing.

'He's cute, isn't he?' Summer looked at Ryan.

'Yeah,' said Marissa. She sounded bored.

'OK, he's not Luke. We know. But he's cute,' Holly laughed.

\*\*\*

'So, you never told me. What do you think of Newport?' Marissa appeared next to Ryan.

Ryan looked around him. 'I think there's less trouble where I'm from,' he said.

'Coop, come here,' Holly shouted.

'I have to go,' Marissa said.

\*\*\*

Outside, Seth was feeling drunk. 'So, this is what it's like. Parties. Girls. Beer. Not bad,' he thought. He got another beer.

\*\*\*

'Newport isn't so bad,' thought Ryan, 'but these rich kids … . In Chino, kids drink because there's nothing else to do. These kids have everything, but they drink too.' He went outside.

Summer saw Ryan. He was standing outside alone. She was quite drunk now. She decided to talk to him.

'Hi,' she said.

'Hi,' said Ryan. He didn't feel comfortable.

'So what's your name?' Summer asked and moved closer. She put her arm round him.

'Ryan.' Ryan felt more and more uncomfortable. He thought about Seth.

'I'm drunk,' Summer said. 'Will you take care of me?'

Ryan moved away as Summer tried to kiss him. Just then Seth came up.

'Ryan, I …' Then he saw Summer. Summer and Ryan. 'What … what are you doing?' he said.

'Seth. Hi,' Ryan said. He moved away from Summer.

'What are you doing? I named my boat after her.' Seth was drunk and angry.

'What? Who are you?' Summer said. She tried to move closer to Ryan again.

'Seth, it's not what you think. She's drunk,' Ryan said.

Summer put her arm round Ryan again.

'Ryan, come on,' she said.

'I don't believe you!' Seth shouted. 'Go back to Chino. Steal another car.'

Now everyone was listening.

'Chino?' said Summer, surprised. She moved away from Ryan.

Marissa looked at Ryan. She was drunk, but suddenly she understood. 'It's all true. Everything he said is true. He stole a car. He was in Juvie … .' She walked back to her friends. Everyone was looking at Ryan.

'I've got to get out of here. Go back to Chino. Leave,' he thought. Ryan walked out quickly.

\*\*\*

Seth walked down the beach. Suddenly Nordlund and Saunders and some of the other guys stopped him.

'Go home, geek,' Nordlund shouted.

'Yeah, who invited you?' Saunders shouted.

Seth wanted to go home, but he didn't know where he was. He didn't want trouble. He was lost and now he felt very drunk. But Nordlund and Saunders were starting to have fun.

Ryan was at the front door when he heard the shouting. 'Seth,' he thought. He ran onto the beach.

'We don't want you here, Cohen,' Nordlund said. Four of the guys picked Seth up.

'I know … I'll never come back. Let me go,' said Seth.

'Too late,' Saunders said. They started to carry Seth to the water.

'Put him down!' Ryan shouted.

Then Luke arrived with Nikki. 'What's your problem?' he asked Ryan angrily.

'You tell me,' said Ryan and he hit Luke. The other guys dropped Seth and ran over. Nordlund tried to hit Ryan. Ryan moved quickly away but then Luke hit him. Then they were all hitting him.

Seth knew he had to do something. He pulled one of the guys off Ryan. He felt strong. Then Ryan fell. A guy hit Seth and a moment later Seth was lying next to Ryan. The guys continued hitting them. Finally, Luke hit Ryan one last time.

'Welcome to the O.C. If I ever see you here again, you're dead. Dead!' Luke shouted and walked away.

Ryan and Seth lay on the beach. For a while, they couldn't move.

\*\*\*

'This is terrible,' Marissa thought. 'Ryan isn't who I thought. He's from Chino.'

She had another vodka. Now more than ever, she wanted to escape. 'Where's Luke?' she thought as her eyes started to close.

\*\*\*

'I don't know what to say. Tonight was … fantastic. You were … totally there for me. You were like Brad Pitt in *Fight Club*! Maybe you could teach me how to fight … And next time, we'll win!' Seth said.

For the first time since he arrived in Newport, Ryan really smiled. They were both in the pool house. Ryan was on his bed and Seth was lying on the floor.

'Summer knows who I am now. Do you think I can tell her about Tahiti?' Seth continued.

'Not yet,' Ryan smiled again. 'I'll never forget tonight,' he thought.

He looked across at Seth, but Seth was almost asleep.

Ryan went outside. He had a cigarette and looked across at the Cooper's house. Where was Marissa? Just then a car stopped outside her house. Summer and Holly got out. They were still quite drunk. They pulled Marissa out of the car.

'I don't believe this,' Summer said. 'Coop, where are your keys?'

But Marissa didn't wake up.

'Her mom and dad mustn't see her like this. They'll kill us!' Holly said.

'Where did Luke go?' Summer asked.

Holly didn't answer.

'We can't wake her parents. What are we going to do?' Summer said. The two girls looked at Marissa. They both had the same idea. They ran back to the car and drove away.

Ryan looked at Marissa. She was lying drunk outside her house. He couldn't leave her there. He walked over and tried to wake her. It was impossible. Ryan picked her up and carried her to the pool house. He put her on his bed and lay down on the floor next to Seth.

'Why does she drink like that?' he thought. 'It's like mom. She drinks to forget. Is it Luke? Her family?'

For the moment, there was no answer to his questions and he fell asleep.

# CHAPTER 7
## Back to Chino

That night Ryan dreamed of Marissa. He dreamed that she was lying next to him. But when he woke, the bed was empty. Marissa wasn't there. And Kirsten was at the pool house door.

'Seth? Seth, are you there?'

Seth sat up. He felt ill. He lay down again.

Kirsten came in. 'Seth. Thank God you're here.' She looked at him closely. 'What happened to your face?'

Seth remembered the fight last night. 'I was in a fight ...' he said.

Kirsten was angry. 'What? Who with? Why?'

'I don't really know. I was drunk,' said Seth. He sat up. 'Maybe I'm still drunk.'

Kirsten couldn't believe it. Her little boy ... in a fight?

Drunk?

'Let's go. House. Now,' she said and pulled Seth to the
door. She looked at Ryan. He knew what she was thinking:
*It's because of Ryan. It's his fault.*

'I can't stay at the Cohens' house now,' he thought
sadly. He got dressed and put his things in his bag. He
went into the house. He wanted to do something nice for
the Cohens. He decided to cook breakfast. He was just
finishing when Kirsten walked into the kitchen. She
wanted to shout at him. She wanted to tell him to leave.
But then she saw the breakfast and she couldn't.

'I usually make breakfast,' Ryan said. 'My mom doesn't
really cook, so …'

'Look, Ryan. I'm sorry. You seem like a nice kid, but …'

'It's OK. I understand.' Ryan looked at Kirsten. 'You
have a really nice family,' he said. Then he got his bag and
went to say goodbye to Seth. Seth was in bed.

'I've got to go,' Ryan said.

'You're leaving?' Seth said. He slowly got out of bed.

'Yeah. I've got to go back to Chino. I have to try and talk to my mom … you know,' he said.

'Cool,' said Seth. 'Not cool. But … well …'

Ryan held out his hand, but Seth put his arms around him. Ryan wasn't sure what to do.

'I'll come down to Chino and visit you,' Seth said.

Ryan didn't say anything. Seth in Chino? He couldn't picture it.

Seth was looking for something. He gave Ryan a map. 'Maybe there's somewhere you want to go. It's good for ideas,' he said.

Ryan smiled at him. 'Thanks,' he said and left the room.

\*\*\*

Marissa was standing outside her house when Sandy and Ryan drove past.

'He's leaving. Will I ever see him again?' she thought. After last night, she didn't care that he was from Chino. 'He rescued me. He's my escape. I'll never forget him.'

'Who will take care of her now?' Ryan thought.

Sandy drove to Chino. They didn't talk. He stopped outside Ryan's house and they both got out. Sandy took Ryan's bike out of the car and looked at Ryan. He didn't know what to say.

'So, thanks for everything,' Ryan said. He turned to walk to the door. Sandy started to follow, but Ryan didn't want him to see inside the house. 'It's OK,' he said to Sandy.

Sandy stopped. 'OK,' he said.

Ryan pulled out his keys and put the key in the door. But the door wasn't locked. Ryan went inside. The house

was empty. There was nothing there. Then he saw a piece of paper with a message from his mom. *Ryan, I'm sorry. I can't.*

Ryan wanted to cry. 'This is the end,' he thought.

Outside, Sandy saw the open door. He knew something was wrong. He walked into the house. Ryan was standing alone. All the rooms were empty. Sandy had no choice.

'Come on Ryan, let's go,' he said.

Ryan turned and followed Sandy back to the car. He didn't want to go back to the Cohens' house. But what could he do? He had nowhere else to go and nobody else to help him. He was alone. No dad, no mom, no Trey. Alone.

What happens next?
Read *The OC: The Gamble* (level 3) in the Scholastic Readers series.

*The OC* **first came on TV in summer 2003 and was a complete hit! Teenagers loved the hot actors, the cool beach parties and, of course, the exciting story. But what happens behind the scenes at** *The OC***? We found out ...**

### It's not the real O.C.!

The crew don't film in the real Orange County. It's too far from Los Angeles where most of the OC team live. In fact, they film in Manhattan Beach which is 45 km north of Newport Beach.

### It's not a day at the beach!

Most of the filming happens inside, even the beach scenes. In the world of *The OC*, every day has to be sunny. So instead, the crew use special lights to make bright sun inside – it's almost impossible to tell the difference.

### The girls get up earlier than the boys!

Looking beautiful isn't easy! The girls come to work earlier because they have to spend more time with the hair and make-up team. The boys have an easier time - just like real life!

---

**What do these words mean? You can use a dictionary.**

actor  scene  crew  relax  director  character  episode

## 4 The director's always listening!

All of the actors have a dressing room where they can relax. Sometimes, director Josh Schwarz listens to the actors' conversations. It gives him ideas for their OC characters. 'If someone says something funny, I try to put it in the show,' he says. 'Rachel Bilson (Summer) watches the TV show *The Golden Girls* with her friends. They each say they're a different Golden Girl character. So, in one episode, Summer and Anna watch *The Golden Girls* together and talk about their favourite characters. Their OC characters become more real.'

## 5 It's a big happy family!

'We're all really good friends,' says Mischa Barton (Marissa). 'We hang out together a lot. At the weekends, I go shopping with the other girls, or we all go to the cinema or have lunch. We always remember birthdays too.'

The boys – Ben McKenzie (Ryan), Adam Brody (Seth), and Chris Carmack (Luke) – all play in the same basketball team. 'Our team isn't doing very well at the moment,' says Ben. 'Adam and I need to practise more, but Chris is really good.'

> **Do you watch *The OC* on TV?**
> **Who's your favourite character? Why?**

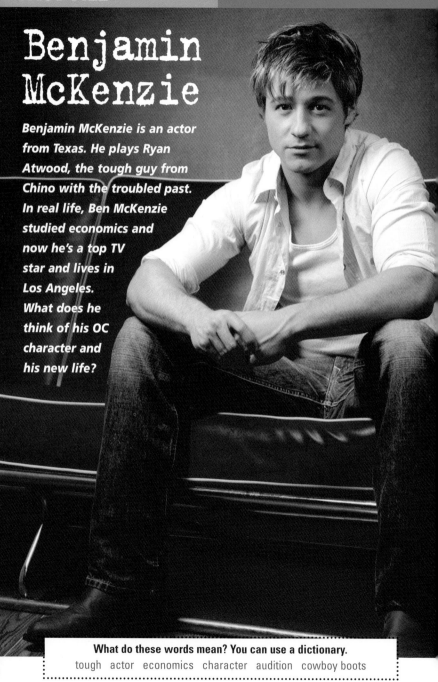

# Benjamin McKenzie

*Benjamin McKenzie is an actor from Texas. He plays Ryan Atwood, the tough guy from Chino with the troubled past. In real life, Ben McKenzie studied economics and now he's a top TV star and lives in Los Angeles. What does he think of his OC character and his new life?*

**What do these words mean? You can use a dictionary.**

tough   actor   economics   character   audition   cowboy boots

## Have you always wanted to be an actor?

No … At school, I was more interested in football! Then I went to university to study economics, and I appeared in a play. It was great fun, and my interest in acting started from there.

## How did you get the part of Ryan?

When I left university, I knew that I wanted to be an actor. After some time in New York, I moved to Los Angeles. During the day, I went to auditions and at night I worked as a waiter. I wasn't a very good waiter – in fact, I was terrible! Then, after about a year, I had the audition for *The OC*.

## What do you think of your OC character?

Ryan's a really interesting character. He has lots of problems because of his past – he can't be open with people easily. He fights first and listens later … He seems tough, but at the same time he feels lost. Ryan always tries to do the right thing – he's a good person.

**Work in pairs. What do you think of Ryan's character?**

## Are you and Ryan the same in any way?

We both like to be alone sometimes. I'm friendly, but I don't want to be around people all the time. I like to have time to think. I think Ryan's the same.

## How are you different?

In lots of ways. Luckily, my family are very different to Ryan's! I had a really happy time at home. And Ryan is luckier with women than me - I can still be uncomfortable with girls now and I'm 26!

## What do you think of L.A.?

I'm from Texas which is very different to L.A. When I first came here, I felt like Ryan in Newport beach! L.A. is full of very rich, strange people! I live in Santa Monica beach now but I never forget where I'm from. I still listen to country music and I often wear cowboy boots! But I like California – I love working on *The OC*.

# The real Newport

Orange County in southern California is famous for sun, sea, and surf! But what do real life teens do in Newport Beach? We asked them!

## 'catch the wave!'

I live to surf and the coolest place in Newport Beach is The Wedge. Surfers from all over the world come here to catch the waves. Sometimes, there are really big waves – as big as the waves in Australia or Hawaii. I always have a fast, exciting ride at The Wedge – you never know when the waves will come.

Joel, 25

Cindy & Grace, 19

## 'we live to shop!'

Our favourite place to hang out is 'Fashion Island'. We drive out there, meet our friends and have lunch at the weekends. We really love Neiman Marcus which has lots of great designer clothes. We love clothes and shopping like Summer and Marissa from *The OC* – but our dads don't lend us their credit cards!

**What do these words mean? You can use a dictionary.**
surf   banana   island   poker   horror

# Beach

Bud & Zoe, 18

## 'Just hang out ..'

I met my boyfriend, Bud, on Newport Pier two years ago. I was working in a café which sold chocolate banana bars. They're very popular in Newport. Bud bought one – and we started talking. We've been together ever since. Now we often go down to the Pier in the evenings. We buy chocolate banana bars, then sit on the beach and watch the waves.

## Newport Beach: the rich and famous

Orange County has always been popular with film stars. In the 1930s, people called Newport Beach 'Little Hollywood' because so many film stars lived there.

## Did you know?

- Humphrey Bogart and Lauren Bacall lived in Newport Beach when they were first married.

- John Wayne lived in Newport Beach when he was a child. The airport in Orange County is called the 'John Wayne Airport'!

- James Cagney owned an island in Newport Bay. He won it in a poker game!

- Michelle Pfeiffer comes from Orange County and she lived in Newport Beach for many years. When she left high school, she was 'Miss Orange County' for a year.

- Horror story writer Dean Koontz lives in Newport Beach. He writes about Orange County in his books.

> **Would you like to live in a place like Newport Beach?**
> **Why / Why not?**

# *Chapters 1–2*

**Before you read**

**1** Complete the sentences with these words. Use the correct tense of the verbs. You can use your dictionary.

**arrest    beer    credit card    get drunk    handcuff    hell
prison    shop assistant    steal    under arrest**

**a)** If you drink too much …, you'll … .

**b)** 'My girlfriend's left me and I haven't got any money. My life is …,' he thought.

**c)** The men … £10,000 from the bank. They ran off before the police could … them.

**d)** The man killed his wife and went to … for twenty-five years.

**e)** 'You're … !' shouted the policeman. He quickly … the man.

**f)** 'Dad. Could you lend me some money to pay my … bill?'

**g)** She worked as a … in a department store in London.

**2** What does 'outsider' mean? A person who …

**a)** usually sleeps outside.

**b)** feels different to other people in a group.

**c)** lives outside a town or city.

**3** Look at 'People and Places' on pages 4–5.

**a)** This book is called *The Outsider*. Who do you think is the outsider? Why?

**After you read**

**4** Complete the sentences with the correct name. (You will need to use some names more than once.)

**Dawn    Jimmy    Julie    Luke    Marissa    Ryan
Summer    Theresa    Trey**

**a)** … lives in Chino and was Ryan's girlfriend.

**b)** … has to get five thousand dollars for some dangerous people.

**c)** … stole a car with his older brother.

**d)** … shouted at his daughter and may be in trouble.

**e)** … 's credit card didn't work when she wanted to buy a dress.

**f)** … wants the best for her daughter, but she doesn't understand her.

**g)** … has been Marissa's boyfriend for six years.

**h)** … is rich, beautiful and bored of life in Newport.

**i)** ... is rich and beautiful and enjoys life in Newport. She's Marissa's best friend.

**j)** ... dreams of having a better life.

**k)** ... drinks too much and has a lot of boyfriends.

**l)** ... lied to her boyfriend for the first time.

**5** What do you think?

    **a)** Will Ryan go to prison or Juvie? What will happen there?

    **b)** Will Luke and Marissa stay together?

# Chapters 3–4

## Before you read

You can use your dictionary.

**6** Which of the words are **a)** people **b)** things or **c)** verbs?

**attorney**    **guard**    **kid**    **nephew**    **probation**    **sail**    **suit**

**7** Complete the sentences with the words from question 7 above. Use the correct form of the verbs.

    **a)** 'It's a beautiful day. Why don't we go ... ?'

    **b)** 'Nice ... !' 'Thanks, it's Armani.'

    **c)** The man didn't go to prison because he had a good ... . He got ... instead.

    **d)** 'He's not old enough to live on his own. He's just a ... .'

    **e)** A prison ... has to work some weekends, evenings and special holidays.

    **f)** 'I love my brother's children, but Jamie is my favourite ... .'

**8** Guess the story. Choose the correct answers.

    **a)** Ryan gets / doesn't get probation.

    **b)** Ryan / A.J. has to leave Dawn's house.

    **c)** Marissa is / isn't going to meet someone new.

    Now read chapters 3–4. Were you right?

## After you read

**9** Are the sentences true or false? Correct the false sentences.

    **a)** Dawn and A.J. have a fight and then Ryan leaves.

    **b)** Kirsten is happy that Sandy has brought Ryan home.

    **c)** Ryan sleeps in the Cohens' pool house.

    **d)** Ryan doesn't think Marissa is good-looking.

    **e)** Marissa invites Seth to the fashion show.

**f)** Seth goes sailing with Summer in his boat *Summer Breeze*.

**g)** Seth doesn't think that Summer will be at the fashion show.

**h)** Seth decides to go to the fashion show with Ryan.

**10** What do you think?

**a)** Will Seth talk to Summer at the fashion show? What will happen if he does?

**b)** Will Ryan see Marissa at the fashion show? What will happen then?

**c)** Will Ryan stay with the Cohens or will he go back to Chino?

# Chapters 5–7

**Before you read**

**11** Answer these questions. You can use your dictionary.

**a)** Where will you find a catwalk?

**b)** What do you use a key for?

**c)** Who do you kiss?

**12** In chapter 6, Ryan and Seth go to a party, and Marissa and Summer are there. What will happen, do you think?

**After you read**

**13** Answer the questions.

**a)** Why does everyone want to talk to Ryan at the fashion show?

**b)** Why does Ryan think maybe life in Newport isn't so perfect?

**c)** Why does Seth tell everyone about Ryan?

**d)** Does Ryan help Seth when he's in trouble?

**e)** Why does Marissa sleep in the Cohens' pool house after the party?

**f)** Why does Kirsten ask Ryan to leave?

**g)** Why does Ryan have to go back to Newport with Sandy?

**14** What do you think?

**a)** How long will Ryan stay with the Cohens? What will happen next?

**b)** Will Marissa find out about Luke and Nikki? Will she and Luke stay together?

**c)** Will Summer notice Seth? Will she and Seth ever be boyfriend and girlfriend?